TALES OF MARTYR TIMES

TALES

OF

MARTYR TIMES

BY THE AUTHOR OF
"THE SPANISH BROTHERS"
DEBORAH ALCOCK

"VINCIT QUI PATITUR."

MOODY PRESS
CHICAGO

Printed in the United States of America

THE MARTYR'S WIDOW

		Page
I.	Danger	9
II.	Martyrdom	20
III.	Victory	27

SUNSET IN PROVENCE

I.	The Two Paths	37
II.	The Page's Story	44
III.	"The Holy War	55
IV.	Conclusion	69

THE CARPENTER OF NISMES

I.	Who He Was	85
II.	Who Were His Friends	93
III.	The Use of a File	101
IV.	A Prison Scene	105
V.	Conclusion	112

A CHILD'S VICTORY

I.	The Shadow of Death	123
II.	The Voice of the Past	131
III.	The End	143

THE MARTYR'S WIDOW

A TRUE STORY

I

DANGER

"Do not fear, Liesken. Our Father cares for me." The speaker was an intelligent and prosperous artisan about thirty years of age. The room in which he sat was plainly but comfortably furnished, not without that air of sober and cleanly quaintness usually associated with the interior of a dwelling in the land of dikes and sandhills. It was late at night, and a lamp burned before him on the table. His young wife, Lisa, stood by his side, her blue eyes filled with tears, and her features shadowed by an expression of anxious care.

"I am sure He does, Carl; but you know He lets those He cares for suffer so often. He lets them be imprisoned — tortured. Oh, Carl," she added with a look of anguish, "He does not *now* 'quench the violence of fire,' as

He did in those old days of which you read to me in the Book."

"No, Lisa," replied Carl, his face lit with faith and courage. "But there still walks with them in the furnace 'one like unto the Son of man.'"

His look at that moment seemed to Lisa a stronger confirmation of her fears than any expression of alarm would have been. She went on almost wildly.

"You are doomed, Carl, and you know it. Since you attended those field preachings last summer twelvemonth, our Burgomaster knows you for a Calvinist, and has had his eye upon you. God help us! In all this blood-stained country, the King of Spain and the terrible Duke have not a servant more willing to aid them in 'wearing out the saints of the Most High' than the Burgomaster of our poor unhappy Gouda."

"He cannot harm me," Carl answered, "until my hour has come, for I serve a mightier King than Philip of Spain — even the King of Glory, the Lord of Life, who hath the keys of hell and of death. See here." He drew a little book from beneath his leather doublet.

But at that moment a low cry proceeded from a room overhead, arousing Lisa to an anxiety more near and pressing, if far less awful, than the horrible apprehension which had just before filled her mind.

Danger 11

"It is our little Franz," she said. Lighting a small lamp she hurried upstairs.

Left alone, Carl opened the volume he held in his hand. It was that treasure of the persecuted Reformed Churches in France and the Low Countries — "The Psalms of David, translated into French verse by Clement Marot." Although Dutch was his native language, Carl, in common with many others of his class, understood French.

In those times it was death, without mercy and without appeal, "to print, write, copy, keep, conceal, buy, or give," any of these books, or any part of them, as well as "to converse or dispute concerning the Holy Scriptures openly or secretly . . . or to read, teach, or expound the Scriptures." The Word of the Lord was precious in those days, and every drop of the water of life which was borne to thirsting souls was like that brought to David from the well of Bethlehem — "the blood of the men that went in jeopardy of their lives."

Yet Carl could not read this night. He was well aware that Lisa's words were true. For months he had gone to his daily work and returned, sat by his fireside, ate and drank, slept and prayed, in the consciousness that any moment he might be summoned from his peaceful home to the dungeon and the stake. Was that a strange life to lead? A solemn one it certainly was, yet it was such a life as thousands led in his country. For a brief space, after years of grinding oppression, the Calvinists of Holland and the adjacent provinces had enjoyed a measure of toleration, they had been permitted to live, under the powerful shadow of the Prince of Orange. Now their protector had himself been forced to flee, and the years of Alva's tyranny had begun — those terrible years, marked evermore in history "with blood and fire, and vapour of smoke." A great cry went up from the bleeding country to Heaven — such a cry as that in Egypt, when "there was not a house where there was not one dead."

Carl was among those who received the truth in the love of it during the interval of comparative quiet. Now he had counted the cost, and held himself prepared, if necessary, to seal his faith with his blood. Yet, were it his Father's will, he would gladly be spared the fiery trial. And who could blame him for this? Had he not Lisa to live for, beside his little fair-haired Franz, pretty Mayken and baby Carl? It was of these he thought as he sat motionless, — his head resting on one hand, while the other still held the psalm-book of Clement Marot. But Carl had acquired a habit. With him thought nearly always changed to prayer, and this constant communion with his Father in Heaven kept

Danger 13

him, as it were, in a quiet place, above the storms of his perilous and uncertain life. He was silently, but very earnestly, laying his fears for those he loved at the feet of Him who cared for him and them, when Lisa hastily re-entered the apartment.

To his inquiry, she answered, "Nothing serious, love. Our little Franz is wakeful and rather feverish. I should like to give him a soothing draught. You need not stir; I have all I want here in the pantry." She moved, lamp in hand, to the further end of the room.

A casual observer would never have perceived the door of this little closet, so carefully was it concealed, and perhaps designedly, being in no way distinguished from the quaint panellings which formed the walls of the room. A panel had to be pushed aside in order to find the way into the dark close recess which Lisa called her pantry — a very inconvenient one, she had often declared and wondered why people built houses in such a senseless manner.

On this occasion she had just begun her search for what she needed, when a thundering knock at the street-door brought her back into the sitting-room, pale and trembling. There was little need for words. Both felt sure the expected trial had come at last. Carl stood before her pale also, but with a flashing eye and an expression of firm determination in his quiet grave countenance and compressed lip.

"It *is*, Liesken —"

"Fly, Carl! oh, fly while you can!"

"It is too late! Whither should I fly?"

Another loud impatient knock, and a sound of rough voices outside.

But a thought, sent as she believed from Heaven into her heart, inspired Lisa with sudden hope and courage. She seized her husband by the arm, and drew him towards the little closet, the door of which she had left open.

"There — in there — fear nothing — I will speak to them."

It was the only plan that offered even a possibility of escape. In a moment more Carl, with the psalm-book still tightly grasped in his hand, was consigned to the dark solitude of the closet. Lisa, after carefully replacing the panel, went forth to meet the intruders, with a silent trembling prayer for strength and wisdom.

And Carl, in his suspense and forced inactivity, prayed also, so earnestly that his whole soul seemed to go up to Heaven in an agony of supplication. His prayer was inarticulate, for words do not come in such moments as these; there are heights and depths in the tried soul beyond their reach. It was not alone or chiefly for himself he feared. A horrible apprehension possessed his mind, that the persecutors, baffled in their search for him, might wreak their vengeance on his precious Lisa, or even on his innocent and helpless children. Such things had been done. Indeed, it would have been difficult to name any deed of violence and atrocity which had not been committed in that hapless country by men who boasted, and often really believed, that these abominations were particularly "acceptable to Almighty God." Fortunately the closet could be opened from within, and Carl stood with his hand on the door, ready to come forth and surrender himself, if necessary. It was well, too, that he could hear the voices from his retreat, first in the passage, and afterwards still more plainly in the sitting-room.

"The Burgomaster is there in person," he said to himself, "I know his angry tones — and he has brought 'Red-rod'[1] with him."

Then he heard Lisa's voice, at first in low deprecating accents, but gradually acquiring strength and confidence. At length, as she stood quite near his place of concealment, he heard her say boldly, "Ye may search the house from garret to cellar, I have said ye shall not find him."

[1] "Red-rod," from the color of his staff of office, was the name given at that time to the officer whose duty it was to arrest criminals and bring them to justice.

Tramp, tramp went the heavy footsteps from the room. Then upstairs. Carl could hear them overhead in the little chamber where his children slept. He could even distinguish the cries of little Franz who had dropped asleep and awoke in terror at the strange intrusion. Now they came down baffled and evidently out of temper they searched the basement story. No, they do not think it worth while to re-enter the sitting-room though the trembling Lisa offered them wine, with the best grace she could. The street door closed heavily. They were gone, thank God! Carl breathed more freely. There was a pause, lest they should return. Then Lisa, slowly and with trembling fingers, attempted to slide the panel back. The momentary strength that danger had inspired forsook her when the strain was over; but Carl's strong hand soon put the barrier aside, and the two stood face to face.

"You have saved me, Lisa," were the first words Carl found power to utter.

"God has saved you, dearest," Lisa answered. She sank on a chair, and looked far paler now than when she confronted the Burgomaster and his officers.

"Then let us thank Him together," answered Carl. He knelt, and in glowing words poured forth his thanksgiving to Him who had just shielded His servants in their hour

Danger

of peril. And fervently did he pray that He would still be with them, to save them if He saw fit, or if not, to strengthen them to suffer all things for His sake. The words were few, but earnest and living, as spoken to One whose presence was a felt reality.

A brief consultation followed Carl's prayer. One thing was now certain. If he wished to see the morrow's sun go down, he must look for safety in flight. This was a last and desperate resource, for the country was so completely overspread by the meshes of a network of tyranny that the unhappy fugitive seemed only likely to run into some fresh danger as terrible as that from which he fled. But no alternative remained. Carl, having made, with Lisa's assistance, some hasty preparations, went to a secret spot where he had carefully concealed the savings of years of industry, such precautions being necessary in those evil times. He took from the little store a few pieces of gold, telling Lisa to use the remainder for the wants of the family.

"And where will you go?" asked the poor wife, as she tried to lay up in her memory the directions he gave, relating to various matters connected with their welfare during his absence.

"It is better you should not know, Liesken, but we shall still have the same Heaven above us, and the same Father to pray to."

He then added calmly and sadly, "I am going upstairs to kiss the children once more." He went up. Mayken and the infant slept, but little Franz was wide-awake, and gazed at his father with large wondering eyes.

"Franz," said Carl, "thy father is going, but thou hast still a Father in Heaven. Trust in Him, boy. Love Jesus Christ thy Saviour, and help and comfort thy mother. Now farewell." He embraced the weeping boy tenderly, kissed the other children without awaking them, and then, with the bitterness of death in his heart, turned to go. Something stronger than a presentiment told him that he should see those loved faces no more. But the hardest parting was to come.

Lisa met him at the door of the sitting-room. "You forgot this," she said, putting the little psalter into his hand, "and you say it always comforts you." Then she added, in a lower tone, as if she feared listeners, "but *the Book*, Carl?"

Carl hesitated a moment, and then he answered firmly, "Keep it, and teach the children to read and love it. Only for my sake and theirs, Lisa, be careful. Never use it until after nightfall, and be sure the doors are bolted. Then no harm can come to you, for its hiding-place is secure — secure as the grave. Now God be with thee, Liesken, my own —"

"And with thee, Carl." A moment more, and Lisa stood alone, the sunshine of her life gone, perhaps for ever. She carefully refastened the door and arranged a few matters which their preparations had left in confusion. Then she sat down and wept, until the dawn of a cheerless December morning aroused her to the consciousness that life, with its struggles, cares, and duties must still go on.

II
MARTYRDOM

"No, Lisa, you must not go out this morning," said old Hans Tiskan the clothweaver, Carl's tried and faithful friend, and himself also in heart a Calvinist. Lisa was standing cloaked and hooded, with a marketbasket on her arm. It was now three months since her husband's departure, and not one word of tidings had reached her. This was not worse than she expected, yet she looked pale and anxious, and her lip quivered as she listened to the unexpected remonstrance.

"But, Hans," she answered, "you know the poor children have no one now to look to but me. Indeed I must go, for their sakes."

Hans Tiskan's lip quivered too, but instead of answering he gently took the basket from her arm, unloosed her cloak and hood, and drew her to a seat. There was something in the strange tenderness that replaced his usually blunt and rough though kind manner, which surprised and even alarmed her. Rather from a vague sinking of heart than any definite cause, her tears began to flow. The old man did not ask her to restrain them. He sat down beside her, took her hand gently in his, and murmured in a trembling voice, "Poor child."

Then he told her, very slowly and gradually, what he knew she must hear. Carl ventured back to Gouda in the hope of obtaining a brief interview with his family and had been recognized the night before by one of the Burgomaster's secret agents. Even while they spoke, he was standing before that relentless judge to answer for the crime of heresy. Hans did not doubt that he would fearlessly confess his faith. There was but one result to look for, a swift and sure one. How could he speak to her of that? It was not necessary. Her own heart divined all.

The crowd in the market-place — the grim angry faces — the silent glances of sympathy and suppressed tears — the execrations and threats of vengeance that sometimes were scarcely suppressed, though it might be death to breathe them — the chain — the stake — the piled faggots — the hideous lurid glare in the sunlight — then the little heap of ashes and the few feet of blackened earth — these were every-day realities to the men and women of Holland three hundred years ago. There was scarcely a Calvinist family in the Provinces that did not number amongst its members one at least who "was not, for God took him" by that chariot of fire to Heaven. Well indeed was it for the mourners, if looking beyond the wrath of man, they could bow their heads and say, "*God* took him," and be thus delivered from the agonizing sense of wrong and the passionate longing for revenge that must have burned like fire in unsanctified hearts.

At first Hans Tiskan's terrible news completely overpowered Lisa, and she found refuge from her sorrow in unconsciousness. When at length she recovered, and was able fully to comprehend her husband's situation, it was very difficult to persuade her she could do nothing to save him. Piteously did she entreat Hans to allow her to go with her little ones, throw herself at the Burgomaster's feet, and beg for mercy.

"Surely he will pity us," she said. "He too has children."

"Thou shalt not go," returned Hans, sternly and bitterly. "Carl's wife shall never kneel to *him*. His heart is harder than this," and he ground his heavy heel upon the hearthstone. "I would that heart were there," he added, muttering the words between his teeth, while the expression on his face told plainly that had the wish been granted, his strong foot would have gone down still more heavily.

It was still more difficult to convince poor Lisa that her desire to see Carl again must not be gratified. Perhaps Hans could scarcely have dissuaded her from making the attempt had she possessed the necessary physical strength, but it was too evident that her trembling limbs could not have borne her through that crowd in the market-place. Yet he must not die without a friend to witness his conflict, and to speak a word of sympathy.

"Go, Hans," she said softly, as he still lingered, trying to comfort her.

Hans laid his hand on his beret. "What shall I tell him from you?" he asked, without looking towards her.

Strength in her uttermost weakness and agony was given to Lisa, and she answered firmly, "Tell him to remember who has said, 'Be thou faithful unto death, and I will give thee a crown of life.'"

"There spoke a hero's wife, — nay more, a martyr's!" said Hans as he went out.

Carl, in the meantime, had witnessed a good confession before his judges. According to the strict letter of the infamous "edicts," not even recantation could save the heretic from the penalty of death, though it would procure a mitigation of his punishment. It would seem, however, that the anxiety of the Romish party for conversions led them not unfrequently to disregard the law, and to offer a free pardon as the price of apostasy. The offer was made to Carl, was even pressed upon him; for his character stood high in the estimation of his fellow-citizens, and rendered his example influential.

"Do you not love your wife and children?" asked the Burgomaster.

"God knows," answered Carl, "that if the whole world were of gold, and my own, I would give it all only to have them with me, even had I to live on bread and water, and in bondage."

"You have them," replied his judge; "only renounce the error of your opinions."

"Neither for wife, children, nor all the world, can I renounce my God and His truth," answered the prisoner.[2]

Nothing remained but to pronounce the sentence and carry it into execution — two things very quickly done. Carl died as thousands did — men, women and even children, a great company.

Of many no record remains, save perhaps some grim entry still visible in the municipal archives, "For having executed so and so by fire, so much; for having thrown his cinders into the river, so much more." Of others,

[2] The dialogue given above actually took place.

touching stories may be gleaned from old chronicles and martyrologies, differing in various particulars, yet always alike in one trait — the sufferers were never forsaken at the last hour by Him in whom they trusted. One unfaltering song of confidence and triumph was on their lips as they died. The annals of the "white-robed army of martyrs" would fill an ample volume, yet there would not be the name of one solitary individual, who, having raised his Master's cup to his lips, found the taste too bitter and refused to drink.

When the chill March evening set in, and the streets of Gouda at last grew dark and quiet, Hans Tiskan entered Lisa's dwelling once more. He brought to her from the lips of the dead words of strength and comfort; and from the loved hand that might touch hers no more on earth, a precious token, the French Psalm-book, with the leaf folded down over the passage,—

> I pass the gloomy vale of death
>   From fear and danger free,
> For there His aiding rod and staff
>   Defend and comfort me.

Having at long intervals and with a faltering voice told her all he knew, he brought her infant, the baby Carl, and laid him by her side; he then sat down a little apart, and "lifted up his voice and wept." *She* did not weep.

And now Lisa was a widow, and her children orphans, the widow and orphans of a martyred Calvinist. In how many obscure homes there wept and agonized such as these!

III

VICTORY

AT FIRST it was not sorrow that overwhelmed Lisa so much as horror, "a horror of great darkness." She could not weep or pray. She could scarcely think. It would have been so easy to lie down beneath the weight of her anguish, to follow Carl and be at rest. And most likely this would have been the end of all had not little hands, strong in their feebleness, drawn her back to life. Carl's children must not starve, however sore their mother's heart might be. So when her husband's store was well-nigh exhausted, the young widow shook off her dreary torpor, and began to toil early and late to supply the necessities of her children. Yet as she toiled, her grief became gradually less agonizing, many a prayer to her husband's God arose from her heart, and many a tear that brought with it healing and comfort dropped upon her work. She well remembered in after times the first gush of tears that were not of unmixed bitterness. It was morning, just after sunrise in late spring or early summer, and already at her task, she plied her needle beside the open window, while the children lay near her asleep in their little cribs. One of those sudden fantastic tricks of memory seemed to transport her in a moment to the quiet corner of a neighbouring churchyard, where there was a little grave, bright no doubt with that early sunshine. An infant she had lost was laid there, and often in happy days — days when she used to call *that* sorrow — she and Carl had visited the spot together, and Carl had spoken to her there of Him who is the Resurrection and the Life. What a sweet resting place appeared that peaceful grave, contrasted with the handful of ashes and the few feet of blackened clay in the marketplace!

"And yet he too shall arise," thought Lisa. His own voice, strong and clear, yet gentle as it had sounded beside his baby's grave, seemed to repeat the blessed words, "I know that he shall rise again at the resurrection of the last day." She bowed her head and wept in silence; but thought while she wept of the glorious morning when the dead in Christ shall be raised incorruptible, and of Him at whose voice they shall come forth, and was comforted. Thus gradually and slowly

> did a succour come,
> and a patience for her grief.

Months passed away and years. There was sorrow, deep and lasting; there was loneliness, but there was not despair. Conflict there was sometimes, when the heart asked wildly why God permitted such things as these to happen upon the earth. "Righteous art thou, O Lord, when I plead with thee, yet let me talk with thee of thy judgments. Wherefore doth the way of the wicked prosper? wherefore are all they happy that deal very treacherously?" "Thou art of purer eyes than to behold evil, and canst not look on iniquity; wherefore lookest thou upon them that deal treacherously, and holdest thy tongue when the wicked devoureth the man that is more righteous than he?" But when these thoughts came, she prayed. She turned to Jesus in humble trust and love, and at last "He arose, and rebuked the wind and the sea, and there was a great calm."

She taught Carl's children "the Book" which he had loved, and from its pages she herself learned many a holy lesson. Nor did she learn in vain, for the Lord Himself was her Teacher, and "who teacheth like Him"?

There was one verse in the Book she thought very difficult: "Love your enemies."

"Love Carl's murderers! does Jesus ask me to do this? It is not in human nature." Then she would remember Him who prayed, "Father, forgive them," and long to feel, or at least to do as He did. But the prayer she tried to offer always died away in words like these, "O Lord, I cannot! O Lord, help me!" And in His own time He helped her.

Lisa never went to mass, never confessed to a priest; her husband's death seemed to put an insurmountable barrier between her and these things, and at the same time to render her nearly callous to the danger she incurred in neglecting them. Even Hans Tiskan remonstrated with her on her imprudence, and tried to awaken her maternal solicitude.

"God will take care of the children," she would answer, "if anything happens to me, as He has taken care of me and them these three years. But let the consequences be what they will, I *cannot* go to the idol worship."

This was the result partly of faith, and partly of utter indifference to life. Its brightness and preciousness were gone forever; she held it very loosely, and only for her children's sake. For some cause or other she was allowed to pursue her course unmolested, although victims as obscure and helpless as she was were being daily sacrificed to the demon of persecution. Her feeble health gave a sort of pretext for her absence from the public rites of the Church. And as none of her children were as yet old enough to take their first communion, the delinquencies of the little heretic household happily escaped observation.

Four years passed away, and then there came a change, a great and happy change for Holland — daybreak after midnight — even though but the dawn of a stormy and uncertain day. The terrible "Sea-beggars" were in the land. They had taken Brill, and the cry of joy that celebrated its capture was a summons to all brave hearts throughout the country to throw off the intolerable yoke of Alva. From town to town the glad tidings passed. "The Beggars are here! The Prince of Orange, the man sent from God to deliver us, is at hand! The hour is come — let us strike for God and freedom."

The men of Gouda heard that cry, and they obeyed. By an irresistible popular impulse, and almost in one hour, the Calvinists had triumphed, and the instruments of Alva's tyranny were trembling fugitives. They had need to fly, for woe to the Spaniard — worse woe to the recreant Hollander in Spanish pay

— who fell into the hands of the enraged townsfolk!

"This for my father, burnt to ashes at the stake — for my brother, who died upon the rack — for my sister, who perished in your dungeons!" With such watchwords as these, it was no marvel that the right hands of the avengers were strong, and their swords went not back from blood. It seemed likely that Hans Tiskan might have his wish fulfilled, and set his foot on the Burgomaster's heart that night.

Terrified at the noise and uproar in the usually quiet town, and wondering what was to be the end of all, Lisa, with the help of little Franz, barred the door and windows securely, and mingled prayers for the dying with trembling thanksgivings for the dream of liberty, as yet too strange and new to seem more than a dream.

A knock at the street door, loud and hasty, yet uncertain, as if the hand trembled that held the knocker, startled the little family. Lisa hesitated to answer the summons, but it was repeated almost instantly, and with still greater impatience.

"Mother, I'll go — I'm not afraid!" said Franz, starting to his feet.

But Lisa took a small lamp in her hand and went herself. She unbarred the door, and looking out into the darkness, inquired what was wanted.

"For God's sake, help — shelter — save me from my enemies!" prayed a voice tremulous with terror.

"Who asks this from me?" said Lisa.

"For God's sake, let me in!" reiterated the fugitive in tones of anguish. "They are coming — here — down this street!"

In his agony of entreaty he advanced one step nearer the half-open door. The light of Lisa's little lamp flashed on his face, pale with fear as it was. She recognized her husband's murderer, the cruel burgomaster!

It cost her no painful conflict *now* to open wide the door, and to say, "In the name of Jesus Christ — come in!"

The invitation was accepted immediately. The fugitive in his terror did not recognize the house, or he would scarcely have chosen it for his place of refuge. Nor did the calm pale face of the young widow strike any chord of memory within. Lisa led him silently across the hall and through the sitting-room; her look checked the eager questions of the children. Something in it awed them strangely.

"Franz," she said, turning calmly to the wondering boy, "bolt the door, and make all secure again."

She then quietly and rapidly slipped back

the panel of the secret closet and signed to the Burgomaster to enter.

"Shall I be safe here?" he asked.

"O yes, sir," answered Lisa, "quite safe. It was here my husband was hid while you and your officers searched the house for him in vain. Enter without fear, your worship; I will be answerable for your safety."

And the martyr's widow kept her word. Very happy was her heart that night, and full of thankfulness her simple prayer. There was no agonizing struggle to be gone through. All that was passed long since — God had given her the victory. He had enabled her to do what Carl would have wished, nay more, what He himself desired; and on her calm brow there seemed to be plainly written His blessing, "Child of your Father in Heaven."

SUNSET IN PROVENCE

A TALE OF THE ALBIGENSES

I

THE TWO PATHS

"I WILL NEVER DO IT, never!"

The breath of these proud words seemed to thrill the banners that hung round the baronial hall of the Count of Toulouse. What was it the young Raymond Roger, Viscount Beziers, declared he would never do, as he stood confronting, almost defying, the powerful head of his house?

"My lord and my uncle may command my service in any lawful war, and my obedience so far as honour and conscience permit."

The old man interrupted him with an angry gesture. "Have the Counts of Toulouse ever asked aught of their vassals contrary to honour or conscience?"

"My lord, I am your sister's son but not your vassal," the youth replied with perhaps unnecessary pride. "But that is not the question," he added sadly and in a gentler tone;

"you counsel me — nay, you *command* me," and he bowed his head slightly at the word, "to submit myself unreservedly to our Holy Father the Pope, in the person of his Legate."

"I do, as thou dost value life and lands. If thy retainers had not infected thee with their heresy, wherefore shouldst thou hesitate?"

"I — the son of Roger Taillefer — a heretic! None of our race were ever that, thank Heaven. But can the Count ask wherefore I hesitate? Not that I fear the disgrace of a public penance, though methinks they might have spared it to the greatest seigneur who speaks the Langue d'Oc[1], and withal so submissive and obedient a Catholic."

The Count's eye fell, and a flush of shame and indignation crossed his face. "Dost thou taunt me with that?" he exclaimed. Then, with an effort, he cleared his brow, and, shrugging his shoulders, said in a tone of studied carelessness, "A knight might spend his days more joyfully in his lady's bower, or on his good steed following the chase, than kneeling at the tomb of some saint of very doubtful repute, with a scoundrel of a monk standing over him scourge in hand. But, nephew, thy hands are pure from the blood of legate or churchman, and for the rest, thou canst plead youth and inexperience.

[1] The dialect of southern France. Allusion is made above to the penance imposed on the Count of Toulouse for the murder of the Papal Legate, Pierre de Castelnau, by some of his retainers.

Draw on thy treasury freely, bribe every one, from my lord the Legate to the lowest acolyte in his train, and I pledge my coat of mail (you know it, of Italian workmanship and inlaid with silver and ivory) you will come off with safety and honor."

"Honor!" repeated young Raymond bitterly. "God keep me from such honor! Can honor survive when mercy and truth are gone for ever? Consider what you ask. Of my retainers — and faithful retainers have they ever been to me and mine — my lord knows that more than half abhor the Mass, and follow the Albigensian and Pateran heresies."

"Then let the slaves abjure their heresies, and obey their lawful lords," said the Count of Toulouse. He spoke with angry impatience, for a consciousness of being in the wrong, which he tried hard to smother, irritated his naturally mild temper, and during the whole of their protracted interview he had been reasoning down his own better self, as well as the generous resolution of his youthful kinsman.

"They ought," returned the viscount, "but the question is, will they? You can answer that! What have you seen in your own territories since the Legate and his satellites have taken the power into their hands, and begun to 'make inquisition for heresy'?"

A change passed over his young eager face

as he added, "And *I* have seen things of which I hardly dare to speak or *think,* lest I should doubt that there is a God in Heaven that sees them too. Tortures, murders, conflagrations, a fruitful land reduced to desolation. The infidel Saracen is a nobler foe than these Crusaders, with the white cross on their arms and every evil passion in their hearts. At least, the infidel fights with *men,* but the Crusader wreaks his direst vengeance on the innocent and helpless — on that womanhood which every true knight should protect at the expense of his heart's best blood — on that childhood which appeals, with the strong cry of its weakness, to all that is human within us. Did they not burn ——"

"It is useless to dwell on atrocities that we all lament," the Count interrupted uneasily.

"But it is not useless to prevent them in future. This much at least I say; before they do such things in the lands of Beziers, the lord of Beziers will sacrifice his life."

"Foolish boy! what would you do? Can you scrape together, out of all your lands of Beziers and Albi, so many as eight or ten thousand men? Yet you talk as if you dreamed of taking the field against a host of three hundred thousand, headed by such chiefs as the Duke of Burgundy and the terrible De Montfort."

"I must defend my people," said the Viscount of Beziers.

"Defend them! that is clearly impossible. Wilt thou perish with them, or wilt thou save thyself while it is still possible?"

Raymond looked steadily in his uncle's face. His own was very pale, but his voice was firm and calm as he answered, "I will perish with them."

"If thou art mad, I am not. The last counsel thou shalt ever have from my lips I give thee now. Leave this place without an hour's delay, lest I find thee quarters in the keep until thy submission is lodged with our lord the Legate, and a branch of our ancient house saved from utter ruin."

"My lord!" exclaimed Raymond in a tone of indignant surprise.

"Go. Do not tempt me too far."

"It is time indeed that I should go, if it be thus the Count of Toulouse honors the ties of blood and friendship, and the solemn bond of a contract he cannot have forgotten."

"Dost thou dare to speak of that contract?" said the angry Count. "It is *thou* who hast forgotten. Could the madman who rushes upon certain ruin dream of claiming the alliance, the hand of ——"

"Forbear, my lord; at least let that name not be named between us," said the youth in a tone of deep emotion, and he turned away his face. A moment afterwards he resumed more calmly, "I must defend the cause of the oppressed. If I fall, I shall at least fall not dishonorably; you need not blush for me. And perhaps when the struggle — the unequal struggle — is over, and the last Viscount of Beziers has died for his people and his rights, Count Raymond of Toulouse may speak of his fate in other terms than he does now, and with a different feeling. Farewell!"

He turned to go, but when he had almost reached the door he looked back for a moment, and added, 'My lord count, the devil does not always keep his promises. Neither do the priests theirs. The security and peace for which you are bartering your conscience may not after all be yours. God grant you do not regret, when regrets are unavailing, that you did not act a nobler part."

He strode from the hall, and his angry, yet in heart half-relenting, kinsman soon heard his voice in the court-yard hastily summoning a favorite page, the only attendant he had brought with him on his rapid and secret journey.

The Count of Toulouse and Raymond de Beziers met no more on earth. The former went to Rome, to seal his disgraceful peace with the persecuting power which was carrying fire and sword into the heart of his fair dominions, and dooming his innocent vassals to a thousand torturing forms of death. The latter, despairing but resolved, took his homeward way with the words on his lips, "I will die with my people!" So their paths divided.

II

THE PAGE'S STORY

THE YOUNG KNIGHT and his attendant rode on in silence amidst the vineyards and the oliveyards of fair Languedoc. War (that worst of all wars, enkindled by fanaticism) had not yet laid its blighting hand on the district through which they passed, and all looked bright and gay in the sunshine of early spring. But in Raymond's soul there was darkness. He had conceived it possible, by an effort of heroic courage, and with the assistance and hearty co-operation of the Count of Toulouse, to turn back the tide of the crusading army, and for this time at least to save his people; but the defection of his powerful kinsman changed the aspect of affairs. Already the cause had become desperate. Now it seemed utterly hopeless; yet with a clear apprehension of the danger, and a resolute though breaking heart, he chose to

THE PAGE'S STORY 45

die rather than abandon it, for he could not desert his vassals, and consent to witness and abet the cruelties of the Crusade and the Inquisition. Still life had high hopes for him. One hope especially there was, closely entwined with the friendship and favor of the Count of Toulouse, with which it was hard to part, how hard might perhaps be revealed by the mute anguish of his gaze as he turned it on the lofty battlements of the castle, ere the winding road concealed them from his view. Then there passed over his face a look of stern, almost defiant resolution; he was arming himself with the courage of despair, but it was armor that tortured while it strengthened — a cuirass worn above a recent wound.

After riding along for some time at a rapid pace, he checked his steed a little, and called, "Henri!"

The page spurred his stout palfrey to the side of his master's horse, and raised his large dark eyes, full of the fire and softness of a southern clime. The boy was of noble birth; it is well known that the office, which his close-fitting jerkin of fine cloth and plumed cap betokened, was considered in that age the most fitting preparation for the duties of knighthood. He looked sad and thoughtful — remarkably so for one so young, but this might have arisen from his evident though silent sympathy with the sorrow of his lord. Ignorant of the business which had brought them to Toulouse, the page formed his own conjectures. Among the retainers of both houses rumors were rife of the proposed alliance between the young Viscount of Beziers and the beautiful and only daughter of Count Raymond VI of Toulouse. When, therefore, the Viscount left his uncle's castle hastily, without ceremony and with a frown on his brow, when no admission was vouchsafed him to the "bower" where the Lady Beatrice and her attendants told their beads, wrought marvelous embroidery, and listened to the *chanzos* and *sirventes* of the troubadors, what could an observant page who loved his master conclude, save that some terrible obstacle — probably a quarrel between the uncle and nephew — had unexpectedly arisen? He was thinking very hardly of the Count, upon whom he of course laid the entire blame, when his lord's voice called him to his side.

"Henri de la Vaur," said he, "thou hast never told me thy history. I know it from others, but would fain hear it now from thine own lips."

"There is but little to tell, my noble lord," replied the boy sadly.

"Thou wert born amidst those grand white mountains yonder?" said the knight, pointing towards a faint white line near the horizon, where the distant Pyrenees might be rather dreamed than seen.

"No, my lord," answered the page. "I have been there with our kindred, at Minerbe, but I was born in our own castle of La Vaur. I scarce remember my father, the lord of La Vaur, he fell in battle more than ten years ago; but my mother, the Lady Girarde — ah, my lord has surely heard of her — she was so beautiful, so good. The poor all loved her, and from her gate was none ever sent empty away. Most gently she comforted those who were in sorrow; most tenderly she ministered to the sick; the orphans were to her as her own children; — she thought of all, cared for all."

Here the boy stopped abruptly, overcome by his emotion. The young Viscount's thoughts reverted to his own beautiful and brilliant mother, Adelaide of Toulouse, whose charms were sung by the most celebrated of the troubadors, in *chanzos* which still exist for the study of the antiquarian. How different from hers was the tranquil life of the Albigensian lady! Yet this had an austere and quiet loveliness, almost more captivating, he thought, than all the glare and glitter of the court beauty's triumphant career.

"I have heard of the good deeds of the

Lady Girarde de la Vaur," he said compassionately. "No doubt they deserve the favor of God, and were not forgotten by Him."

Henri looked perplexed, and after some moments' thought, he answered modestly and in a low voice, "I am sure God has not forgotten them, my dear lord. But she always *knew* He loved her, and had forgiven her sins for the blessed Saviour's sake. She did these things only because her heart thanked Him for His grace and love, and she longed so much to please Him. All her life was one great song of thankfulness, like those grand old hymns you sing in chapel, high and holy yet so sweet." He paused, but the Viscount said, "Go on, Henri."

"At last," he resumed, "there was a rumor of war in the land, and our people said to each other in terror that the Crusaders were coming. Our castle of La Vaur could not well be defended, and we had but few fighting men amongst our retainers, but my mother's brother, the noble Lord Almeric, a brave and skillful captain, came to our help, and encouraged us to do our best and hold out to the last. Our attendants also (who were all of our own faith save old Gaston the seneschal) were well armed and courageous, so it seemed best to us to put our trust in God and to strengthen our fortifications to stand a siege. Scarce had we finished this work when

The Page's Story

the Crusaders came. It may be we might have wearied them out, but alas! our supply of provisions failed! What could we do? My uncle and his knights deemed it wisest to surrender, making such terms as they could with the besiegers. Would to God they had said like King David, 'better to fall into the hands of the Lord God than into the hands of man!'

"That fatal morning, when the castle gates were thrown open to our enemies, my mother and I sat alone in our apartment. Defense and flight were alike impossible, and as it was thought best to avoid all show of attempting either, she would not allow even our personal attendants to gather round us. We clung close together, listening to the cries and the tumult outside, and for a long time we did not speak.

"At last she said, 'Let us pray to God.' She knelt and prayed, 'O God our Father, strengthen us to witness for Thy name, and if it be Thy will, take us quickly home to Thee, through the merits of our Saviour Christ.' Then she rose and stood beside me, looking very pale but calm. I still knelt, she laid her hand on my head and said in a firm voice. 'My son, promise thy mother thou wilt never deny the Lord thy Saviour.'

"I answered, 'Mother, I promise'; and she bent down and kissed my brow, a long burning kiss, — I feel it still, — it was her last." He paused for a few moments and then continued with at least outward calmness, "I know not how long it was ere the door was rudely thrust open, and some six or seven fierce-looking Crusaders rushed in, the foremost had an axe in his hand, there was blood upon it, and I mind me the white cross on his arm was streaked with blood.

" 'Yield, heretics!' he cried, brandishing his weapon.

"My mother said, 'We yield, only lead us without voilence to your general.' The wretch sprang forward and seized her arm as if to drag her with them. I threw myself on him and struck him with all my might."

"Bravely done, boy! Well?"

"He raised his axe. The room seemed to fall on me. I knew no more. When I regained consciousness it was night, the moonlight lay on the floor in long, narrow streaks. I was alone. The only thought that found place in my mind was this one, 'Where is my mother?' I tried to stand, but felt strangely weak and faint, and putting my hand on the floor beside me found it was wet with blood.

"At last I managed to rise, and with great difficulty succeeded in clambering up to the high narrow window, which looked out on the courtyard. What a sight met my eyes! All below me looked black in the moonlight —

The Page's Story

frightfully black! Fragments of wood and other rubbish half consumed by fire covered the ground — and amongst them, gleaming hideously, white, there were — there were ——"

"Of what horrors dost thou speak?" cried Raymond.

"My lord," returned the page, "in that court-yard they burned to death, in one great fire, more than a hundred men and women. Besides these were eighty persons hanged on lofty gibbets, among them my noble Uncle Almeric. 'Shall I not visit for these things, saith the Lord?'" and the boy's breast heaved, and his slight form seemed to dilate with the passion that filled his soul.

"Better to cast in my lot with thee than with them," said the young Viscount thoughtfully to himself. He added aloud, "But thy lady mother, what of her?"

"Not *there*, my lord," said the page.

"A vague, nameless, horrible dread came over me at what I beheld. I tried to cry aloud, but something choked my voice, and letting go my hold of the window, I fell to the ground and again lost consciousness. How long I lay thus I know not, but it was still night when I felt some one touch me, and heard old Gaston's voice. I whispered, 'Gaston, tell me in pity where is my mother, does she live?'

"His answer was, 'She lives, come with me, I will take you to her.' God forgive him! but the lie saved my life, for the hope it brought me sent new strength through my feeble limbs. He bound my wound, gave me a draught of water, threw a cloak round my shoulders, and led me through the long passages to a small private door of the castle. There a man, also wrapped in a cloak, stood waiting with two horses. Gaston exchanged a few words with him too low for me to hear, and put something into his hand. Then we mounted, and as Gaston did so, I saw in the moonlight that he wore the hateful white cross. When the sentries challenged us, he gave them the pass-word of the night ('The wounds of St. Sebastian,' I think it was) so we rode away safely, and being mercifully preserved through many dangers, at last we reached your town of Beziers, where my noble lord so kindly and generously took us under his protection."

"But how could Gaston induce one of those pitiless wretches to aid your escape?" asked the Viscount.

"By discovering to him the place where my mother had concealed her jewels," answered Henri. "My lord knows that Gaston, himself a Catholic, ought to have been in no danger; but they were so fierce and cruel that he would have been dragged to death in spite, as he hath it, 'of all the blessed saints in Paradise,' as well as of his own earnest protestations that he was neither an Albigense nor a Pateran, nor of any sect whatever, had not a captain, under whom he once served against the Moors in Spain, rescued him from the fury of his soldiers. And then he witnessed all, *all* the fearful scene. He stood near my dear mother when she answered for her faith and chose death rather than life at the price of forsaking her Saviour. Oh, why was I not there? Why did God deny me the grace to die with her?"

"Because thou wert too young to die, poor child," said his master kindly.

"Oh, no, my lord; boys younger than I have died ere this for the name of Christ. They allowed Gaston to come near enough to speak with her. She said God was with her, and she was not afraid. Then she added low. 'Remember the charge I gave thee.' That charge was to save me. She put into his hand for me a string of pearls that she always wore round her neck, and a little book more precious than pearls or gold. Then they led her away to death. Gaston kept beside her to the last, and saw the end. She was stoned." But the boy's voice was choked by emotion, and he was unable to proceed.

"Henri de la Vaur," said the Viscount in a tone of deep feeling, "God helping me, I will sheathe my sword in the hearts of these miscreants. I swear it."

The page looked up in surprise. "My lord will not, cannot fight with the Crusaders?"

"I must do that thing," returned Raymond, "or give up thee, my child, and all the men women and children who hold thy faith, to be dealt with as were the people of La Vaur. I have heard enough, boy. Thou hast given me what I needed — a thought to nerve my arm in the conflict and to make my heart hard and wild with vengeance, as it should be for such a struggle."

Then there was silence again between the knight and his attendant, and the page dropped once more into his place behind; and as he did so he murmured to himself, "'And Jesus said, Father, forgive them, for they know not what they do.' Merciful Saviour, teach him in Thine own time and in Thine own way."

III

"THE HOLY WAR"

SOME MONTHS ELAPSED since the Count of Toulouse and the Viscount of Beziers parted in wrath and for ever. The young Viscount spent the greater part of them in preparations for a heroic struggle against overwhelming odds. Leaving his capital town of Beziers in the care of his lieutenants, he shut himself up in Carcassone, determining to await the enemy there, and prolong his resistance to the last. But in the month of June horrible tidings reached him, which wrung, though they could not shake, his steadfast heart. The Crusaders had taken Beziers by assault,[2] and put all who were found within its walls, to the number of sixty thousand, to the sword, without distinction of age, of sex or of creed. When the ferocious Arnaud, abbot of the Cistercians, was reminded that there were many good Catholics

[2] June 22, 1200.

in the town, and asked by what means might they be distinguished from the heretics, his answer was, "Kill them all; God will know who belong to Him." And the hideous command was fulfilled to the letter.

A few strong and simple words from a contemporary Provencal historian, himself a Roman Catholic, give a striking picture of the scene: — "They entered the city of Beziers, where they murdered more people than was ever known in the world; for they spared neither young nor old, nor infants at the breast. They killed and murdered them all, which being seen by the said people of the city they that were able did retreat into the great church of St. Nazarius, both men and women. The chaplains thereof, when they retreated, caused the bells to ring until everybody was dead; but neither the sound of the bells, nor the chaplains in their priestly habits, nor the clerks, could hinder all from being put to the sword. Only one escaped, for all the rest were slain and died. Nothing so pitiable was ever heard of or done. And when the city had been pillaged, it was set on fire; so that it was all pillaged and burnt, as it appears to this day. No living thing was left, which was a cruel vengeance, seeing that the said Viscount was neither a heretic, nor of their sect."

After this frightful event, the whole strength of the crusading army, numbering about three hundred thousand men, was turned against Carcassone. For some time Raymond held out, like a wild boar brought to bay by its pursuers — despairing yet dauntless. At length there shone upon his arms one of those transient flickers of success that sometimes light a dying cause. Despair is strong and more than once or twice the sallies of the brave garrison spread dismay through the mighty host whose tents lay white upon all the surrounding plain.

The chiefs of that host — the Duke of Burgundy and the Count of Nevers — as well as the crafty Legate and the fierce De Montfort — began to allow to each other that this young Viscount of Beziers was no contemptible adversary. Whispers of a possible accommodation began to be heard, and the more readily since such a measure need cost the Crusaders but little, the views of Rome upon the necessity of keeping faith with heretics being proverbially lax. Time was precious, and pledges and promises were easily given.

Besides all this, the King of Arragon, Pedro II, who accompanied the crusading army, was a friend and relative of the Viscount, and now showed a disposition to interfere on his behalf. He actually procured an interview with him, and returned to the camp deeply impressed by his gallant and generous spirit, and the manly eloquence with which he maintained the righteousness of his cause.

But the Legate turned a deaf ear to his warm intercessions, and the only grace which the priests who governed the army would offer the people of Carcassone was a permission for thirteen of their number, including the Viscount, to leave the city — the remainder to expect the fate of the people of Beziers. History has preserved Raymond's answer to this proposal. "I would consent," said he, "to be flayed alive, rather than abandon a single one of my fellow-citizens." And "he persisted in defending himself with unconquerable valour."

But renewed offers of accommodation were made; the Crusaders lowered their tone, and seemed to become far less insolent and overbearing. "If the Legate and the Viscount could only meet," they said, "they would be able mutually to satisfy each other, and all would be well."

Finally, the Legate sent an officer of rank into Carcassone, to urge this proposal upon the Viscount, offering him a full safe-conduct for himself and his attendants, secured by the most solemn oaths. Raymond, after much deliberation, agreed to visit the camp, probably considering that the presence of the friendly and powerful King of Arragon was a sufficient guarantee against any meditated treachery.

Early in the morning on the day appointed for the Viscount's interview, the Legate, arrayed in a sort of knightly deshabille, sat before a small table at the upper end of a large hall. Piles of lances and other weapons occupied the lower part, pieces of armor were scattered around, and soldiers, citizens, and servants passed to and fro. Upon the table lay his own morion and steel gloves, and a very beautiful sword with a jeweled hilt and scabbard, while a flask of rare wine and some coarse black bread contrasted with these and with each other.

The young champion of the Albigenses sat buried in profound thought, his head resting on both hands, and his face concealed from view. It was not without counting the cost that he had taken up arms for that persecuted people. From boyhood his mind had been exercised upon the problem of their infidelity, heresy, or *faith,* as he had learned at last to call it. The necessity, early imposed on him, of thinking and acting for himself, gave stability and self-reliance to his character, whilst the existence of a numerous body of men among his vassals who, like himself, were of a reasoning and reflective cast of mind, contributed to stimulate these faculties to still more effective exercise. And now that the crisis had arrived, and that he went forth to plead the cause of his people before a judge that he well knew to be both perfidious and relentless, he was gravely weighing all the probabilities of the case. Notwithstanding his precautions, he might be the victim of some secret snare, he and the band of gallant men, his best and bravest, whom he deemed it his wisest course to take with him. What if they never returned to Carcassone? Should he draw them too into this peril? Yes—if he played his game, it behooved him to play it fearlessly. Mercy and truth might yet be found in yonder camp, and fair terms be obtained for his vassals. Of his own life he scarcely thought; except as involving the one great question of their deliverance, he regarded it with mournful, even with bitter indifference. But was it well to die in conflict with holy Mother Church? Who would raise the crucifix before his eyes, and touch his cold forehead with the sacred oil? He must not, however, in this his hour of action, lose himself again in that sea of confused contradictory thought. God's law and the Church's law being as he believed in conflict, he chose to abide on God's side and to take the consequences.

"Oh, all-merciful!" was the cry that arose from his heart, "to Thee I appeal. Stand by me while I strive for mercy and truth—

stand by me if I fall in that sacred cause. I ask it in the name of Thy Son, the ever-merciful." He raised his head slowly, and saw his page, Henri de la Vaur, beside him.

"My lord," said the boy, "the good father Sicard waits without."

"Let him enter," returned the Viscount. "I sent for him."

Henri ushered in a venerable man with gray hair and beard, in plain dark attire. He bowed to the Viscount and stood in silence, awaiting his pleasure.

"Well, Barbe," said Raymond, "what news?"

"None, my lord, save that our people pray day and night that He who keepeth Israel may keep you beneath the shadow of His wings."

"Dost thou hear them murmur at our strict economy of food?"

"Nay, Viscount, it would ill beseem them. Life could be sustained on far less than we consume, and were it otherwise, every man, woman, and child, among us would perish with hunger rather than open our gates to the enemy!"

"Brave words, Barbe, and not spoken at random either. Now hearken. I go forth today to make terms, if so it may be, not for myself, but for thee and thy people. I pledge my knightly word that neither threat nor promise shall sever my fate from theirs and thine. Dost thou trust me?"

"I do, so help me God!" said the old pastor with deep feeling. "May He reward thee, and He surely will."

A look of emotion passed over Raymond's face. "Thy people have ever dealt well with me and mine," he said, stretching out his hand.

Father Sicard took it and raised it to his lips, while he said with great earnestness, "Would that my good lord could say, 'Thy people shall be my people, and thy God my God.' Would that he knew that precious faith which can keep the heart at peace in the midst of peril, suffering, death itself — that he knew *Him* who is at once the author of that faith and its objects, — then indeed the worst that could come, would but change his coronet into a crown of glory, that would shine for ever and ever."

The Viscount was silent and turned away his face, but the page Henri unconsciously drew closer, and fixed his large dark eyes, first on the speaker, then on his beloved young master with an expression of earnest entreaty.

At last Raymond said, with a smile and rather lightly, "So thou wouldst make me a heretic, Sicard. 'Twere more to the purpose if thou and thy brethren would return to the true Church, and save much blood and many tears."

But the last words were spoken gravely, and a sad and thoughtful look replaced the smile.

"Barbe," he added after a pause, "I summoned thee as a man of sense and intelligence, and one respected by thine own people. I have a secret to confide to thee — Henri, fetch hither a lantern."

The boy obeyed. Raymond took it from his hand and led away the pastor, forbidding Henri by a gesture to follow them. A considerable time elapsed before he returned, then he came alone, having dismissed Sicard.

Henri ventured to ask as he passed, "Is it my lord's pleasure that I should attend him to the camp?"

"No, my poor little heretic," returned the Viscount kindly, "those wild Crusaders would matter little tearing thee to pieces in their zeal for mother Church, so should I lose the best page a knight ever had."

Something in the lord's manner, both to the Pastor Sicard and to himself, touched the boy deeply. "He never used," he thought, "to give his hand to one of our people, and then his words are so gentle — it seems like taking farewell of us." His face flushed, then grew pale again as he knelt quickly at the feet of his master. "A boon, my noble lord, a boon ere you leave us."

"Speak boldly, my child. God knows it is little I have to give, but thou art welcome to the best. What is it? A sword? A good steed?"

Henri drew a strange-looking little volume from beneath his jerkin. It was clasped with gold, and the covers were curiously chased and adorned with the same precious metal. So small were its dimensions that it might have been worn, as such treasures have been, set in a brooch upon a lady's breast.

"Will my lord condescend to take this with him? It will do him good."

"Well, boy, if it please thee. Certainly it will do me no harm. I thank thee." And he took the little book in his hand and examined it curiously. "Hath it the virtue of a talisman, thinkest thou? Will it turn aside the brand or the lance in the day of battle? Or will it give me good success in the business upon which I now go forth?"

Henri rose up well pleased. "I do not know, my lord," he answered simply. "In truth I have never thought; but it does the *soul* good, for it tells of Jesus, the good Saviour, who loves us."

"All these people's religion consists in a fervent faith in Christ, and a strong persuasion of His love to them," thought Raymond, "and that, it seems, is heresy. Passing strange!" He added aloud, "And now, Henri, take my sword *Joyeuse,* and make him as bright as thou canst. Time presses."

The next day there was bitter weeping and wailing in Carcassone. The brave young chieftain returned no more from that fatal camp, the dark abode of treachery and violence. Long did the townsfolk watch and wait, anxiously keeping hope alive in each other's hearts. But when the sun of the second day reached its meridian, and no message or token came from the camp, even the strongest-hearted felt they were abandoned to their fate.

The Albigenses would have been more than human had not a few voices been raised to accuse their absent lord of a faithless desertion of their cause. But the murmur was hushed at once. "He would never forsake us — never," said they all. "His heart is true as steel. But alas! by this time he does not live, or only lives a captive."

Then wilder and louder grew the voice of weeping. The people of Carcassone seemed already to behold the swords of the Crusaders, red from the slaughter of Beziers, at their breasts. Husbands clasped their wives, and parents their children. "God help us, we must die!" they murmured in their despair. But from many hearts in that hour of anguish there arose the cry, "We are Thine, O Saviour Christ — receive us!"

Above the sobbing and the praying of the crowd gathered in the market-place arose a calm clear voice, speaking hope.

"My children," said the Pastor Sicard, "do not abandon yourselves to despair. It is true that we cannot continue to defend the city, yet with God's good help, we may still be saved. Our noble Viscount, ere he left us, revealed to me the entrance to a secret passage, winding beneath the fortifications, and afterwards under ground till it reaches the castle you know of, three leagues on the right hand of our town. Let us wait until the darkness of night makes it possible for our soldiers to leave the ramparts unobserved. Let us kneel once more in the church at the door of which I stand, and there commit ourselves to the merciful protection of Almighty God. Let us then escape thither, and thence we can go forth in His name, whithersoever He may please to lead us; for the whole earth is His, and the fulness thereof."

Eager murmurs amongst the crowd greeted the pastor's proposal. "God be praised. — He has not forsaken us!" was the first thought of those humble and pious sufferers for their faith. And the foremost men among them added words like these: "Father Sicard is

"The Holy War"

right; he is a good man, we will all follow him."

At the dark midnight hour the sorrowful remnant of the Albigenses set out on their perilous journey, taking with them provisions for three days, and in a few instances, such valuables as they could conceal about their person. It was a silent melancholy procession. Mothers carried their infants in their arms, fathers led their little children by the hand. The sick and aged were borne by their friends, with all the care and tenderness that circumstances permitted; for suffering had not made these poor people hard and unfeeling towards each other.

Almost at the last moment Sicard missed Henri de la Vaur, who in the early part of the evening had made himself very useful. He remembered having seen him in the church, and hastening thither, found him still kneeling, his earnest face raised upwards and his hands clasped in prayer. He bade him in a tone of authority rise immediately and follow him.

Henri rose, but said very calmly, "I am praying for my master, and I wish to stay here until the Crusaders enter the town, that if he be a captive they may allow me to go to him and serve him."

"Nay, my son," replied the pastor; "it is a foolish, though a brave and generous thought.

They would murder thee, or force thee perchance by torture to deny thy faith. It is wrong to *seek* such peril, though we should face it bravely when God sends it. Come."

But Henri still hung back.

"This delay may ruin us all," said Sicard sternly. "Yet I leave not this spot without thee; for," he added, "there is none in all the city whom *he* would rather save."

"I go, then, my father," said Henri; but he murmured in a low voice, "I shall see my dear lord yet, for all that"; and the boy's pale, resolved countenance struck the aged pastor. They both rejoined the band of fugitives, which immediately began its dreary march; and thus it happened that when the morning's sun rose in glory over the city, it shone upon deserted ramparts and empty houses. Not a living soul was left in Carcassone. Vainly had Raymond of Beziers been entreated to save himself, and leave the men of Carcassone to perish. He would not have it thus, therefore another lot was appointed him. *He* fell, but they were saved. And it was better so for him.

IV

CONCLUSION

The snow fell in Beziers, covering, with its spotless veil, as if in pity, the charred and blackened ruins, and the streets where so lately blood had flowed in rivers. All was desolation there, made only more dreary by the troops of rough and fierce Crusaders who trod the streets, and occupied such of the dwellings as the fire left habitable — dwellings which once were *homes*, but which were now more in common with the dens of wild beasts. For having killed, the spoilers also took possession. But little joy or profit did such possession bring. The arms of the "white cross host" only availed them to pull down and to destroy; their commission was not in any sense to restore or to rebuild.

The castle of Beziers shared the fate of the town. Plundered, dismantled, and partly destroyed by fire, the favorite residence of the young Viscount — where the proud Roger Taillefer held his court, and the Troubadors sang the praises of the beautiful Adelaide of Toulouse — was now only fit to be used as a prison. The cruel and perfidious De Montfort, whose services to the cause had been rewarded by a grant of the broad lands of the captive Viscount, set little value upon such a residence. Sufficient for his purpose if its gloomy walls were still strong enough to keep, not a crowd of ignoble heretics awaiting their doom, but some political prisoner of importance. The fierce-looking band of Crusaders who guarded it night and day seemed to indicate that it was being employed for such a purpose, especially as they wore, in addition to the white cross on their arms, the badge of the private retainers of De Montfort.

A bare-footed friar, habited in a coarse serge gown, and with his beads in his hand, passed out of the castle. The group of soldiers gathered round the entrance made way for him obsequiously, for he was no less a person than the celebrated Izarn, "Dominican missionary and inquisitor." He looked up from his rosary to mutter a benediction upon them. As he did so, his eye was caught by that of a man in a rich dress, who stood a little apart, conversing with a young lad, apparently a page or messenger from some chieftain of rank.

"Your blessing, holy father," said the captain, for such he was, uncovering his head.

The friar drew near to him.

"The De Montfort has a faithful servant in you, captain," he observed in the *Langue d' Oc*, and with a keen glance that gave some sinister meaning to his words.

The soldier's eye fell; he seemed to relish the commendation but little. He asked hastily, and in the same language,

"Does the prisoner become more docile to your pious instructions, father?"

"Never a whit," returned the friar angrily; "he is obstinate as any of that accursed race with whom he has allied himself." He added in a whisper, "And he will *die* unreconciled to the Church."

"*Die*, father!" repeated the captain uneasily, changing his position.

The friar laid his hand on his arm.

"Come, we understand each other," he said. "He is dying, captain. You best know how. Of a broken heart, *we shall say*."

The captain raised his eye-brows, shrugged his shoulders, and remarked with a little hesitation, 'Yet is it a pity, father, were it not for the sake of Holy Church. So young, and of such noble lineage; gentle too, and courteous, and bearing himself throughout with most undaunted courage."

A sneer passed over the Dominican's hard face.

"It is full late," he said, "for *thee* to talk of pity, save to blind some idiot who knows no better. Thou dost pity, as the hawk pities the sparrow!" He seemed about to turn away, then added aloud, "Who is that boy?"

"An old retainer of the prisoner's, father, who prays that he may go and minister to him. Believing it to be the will of Holy Church that all possible gentleness and mercy should be shown, I have given him permission. Forgive me, father, if I have erred in this." The good captain did not think it necessary to add that the young suppliant had enforced his entreaties by the gift of two large pearls of considerable value.

"*Absolvo te*," said the friar with a grim smile. "But is it *safe*, my friend? Such as he have ofttimes sharp ears and long tongues."

"I risk that," answered the soldier. "Easier to enter these walls than to quit them," and the friar passed on.

A few moments more, and Henri de la Vaur had obtained the desire of his heart, that for which he had braved many perils and endured many hardships. He stood once more in the presence of his lord the Viscount of Beziers. He stood in his presence, yet he saw him not. Mastering the rush of emotion which brought the tears to his eyes and drove the color from his cheek, he gazed around the dreary comfortless hall. The Viscount there, and neither to speak to him nor to call him to his side, there was something in this so strange that it chilled his heart. At last he saw the object of his search at one end of the room, reclining on a crude couch covered with a piece of tapestry which had been torn from the wall.

Another moment found him on his knees beside him, pressing his hand to his lips. "My dear master!" he murmured in a choking voice.

The once proud and fiery-hearted young knight opened his eyes languidly, and fixed them on him, but did not speak. His face was worn and pale, but its expression, though mournful, was calm and not unhappy; it told of past rather than of present suffering.

"Do you not remember me, my good lord!" said the boy.

"Henri? Yes," Raymond answered softly. "Yes, my child, I remember thee. But old faces come to me so often now, as I lie here betwixt sleep and waking, that I doubt if this be not also a dream."

Worn out by anxiety and by toil, the boy could restrain his tears no longer. Hiding his face in the tapestry of the couch, he wept and sobbed aloud for some minutes. He feared this was the worst thing he could have done; but it proved the best, for it roused the dying man from his torpor.

Half raising himself, Raymond laid his wasted hand on the boy's head, saying gently, "Poor child, do not weep. More help and comfort than thou canst know have come to me in these dark hours. Look here," and with his other hand he sought for something on the couch. It was soon found, and light flashed through Henri's tears as he recognized his own gift — his mother's little book, the Gospel of St. John.

"But by what strange chance art thou here?" asked the Viscount, with something like a return of his natural animation of manner. "Art thou also a prisoner?"

"I came of my own free will to seek my good and kind lord, and to share his fortunes," answered Henri.

Raymond's large languid eyes filled with tears. He did not speak, but raising himself with much difficulty he drew the boy towards him and embraced him. "Brave and faithful child," he murmured at last, "thou dost love on still, when the rest — I deemed myself forgotten by all the world."

Henri knew how to strike a chord sure to respond to his touch. "My lord," he said, "the remnant escaped from Carcassone are safe and trust to make good their retreat to another land."

Conclusion

Raymond's features brightened. "Thank God! then all has not been in vain. Hath any man assumed the command amongst them?"

"Yes, my lord; they all consent to obey the good Pastor Sicard."

"It is well. Where one man knows to command, and the rest obey, there is hope. Thou didst leave Carcassone in their company then?"

"But with the settled purpose of quitting them, and returning to you as speedily as I might."

"Did they know this purpose of thine?"

"I dreamed of stealing away in secret lest they should hinder me. But this plan seemed ungrateful to Sicard, who loved me as a father. So I confided all to him."

"And he tried to dissuade thee, I warrant."

"Well, at first he feared I should never succeed in reaching your — the place where you were."

"My *prison*," said Raymond, with a smile of resignation, more sad than Henri's tears.

"But when I told my plan, and explained how I would bribe the soldiers to give me what I wanted, he yielded, and blessed me and prayed God I might prosper. And then the people came round me, and I think they would have had me take all the gold and jewels they had amongst them; and some wanted to go with me, but that would only have been more danger and no help, for the soldiers do not care for a boy like me so much as for a grown man, and even the monks think I am the servant of some lord or knight, and not an Albigense or a heretic. As for the gold, they pressed it upon me so much that I took a few marks to pay my charges by the way, but for gaining my will from these Crusaders I have what is better than gold." And he cautiously drew from beneath his jerkin what had been a string of fine pearls, but the string was broken, and more than half the pearls were gone.

"Thou hast given all for me, poor child," said Raymond.

"And has not my good lord given all for me and mine?" answered the boy through his tears. "Our people would have sacrificed their lives to serve you," he added. "Words cannot tell how they mourned for you."

"May God preserve and prosper them," returned Raymond. "As for thee, my child, it is good to have thee with me, and to know that a friendly hand will close my eyes. Do not grieve that my hours are numbered. My captivity has not been so sweet that I should greatly regret its close. And this must have come sooner or later. The De Montfort could never have enjoyed his domains in peace whilst Raymond Roger de Beziers lived."

"It is he then who hath done this thing!" said Henri, starting.

"Be calm, my child," answered Raymond, gently. "Thou seest I am calm. Thy Book hath taught me, 'In my Father's house are many mansions'"; and he looked upwards, his face lighted with a beautiful expression of hope and confidence.

"You have found the Saviour then," said Henri, his own heart raised and awed into a calmness like that of the sufferer.

"I think He hath found me," was the low reply, and he murmured half to himself, "Jesus heard that they had cast him out, and — *He found him* — the words are in thy Book." He paused from exhaustion, and pointed to the table. Some wine lay upon it, which Henri brought, but he refused it, and asked for water, saying, "Beware of that wine, Henri — taste it not, touch it not, it would harm thee" — words which Henri did not fully comprehend until long afterwards. After a short rest, he continued, "When first they led me here, a captive, I earnestly prayed that I might receive the holy rites of the Church. Upon one condition alone would the priests grant my prayer. I must acknowledge my sin in having resisted their arms."

"And that you would never do, my lord."

"Could I come before Him who is the truth with a lie on my lips? Purchase the right to partake of His holy sacrament by a frightful sin? God forbid! — They declared me a heretic, excommunicated. Henri, thou canst not tell how it was with me then. All my life I had leant upon the Church, trusted in her aid, and now she forsook me, and I found myself *alone,* a naked soul trembling in the presence of my God, with death beside me, and all the sins of my youth rising up before my face. Men have never called me coward, yet I own that *then* I shivered in intolerable dread. Once it crossed my mind that since the Crusader believes that if he fell in battle with the Albigense, the gates of paradise would open before him and all his sins be blotted out, my conflict for truth and right might also be accepted by a righteous God. But I felt the thought an unutterable absurdity. As if I should say, 'Behold, I have misspent my life, but I have given it at last in Thy cause,' — would He accept it at my hands? There was no help for me there — anywhere. At last I turned to thy Book, for I said, 'Let me read of Him with whom I have to do, that I may know if a man dare to hope in His mercy.' And then I read of the blessed Saviour, — with strange, glad surprise I learned that He is no awful Judge, but the merciful and loving One, the Lamb of God who beareth away the sin — the sin of the world — *and mine*. Alas, my strength fails, I cannot tell thee all."

He had told enough, however, to fill the simple heart of Henri with gratitude and joy.

"It is well with me now," he continued. "He hath said, 'Peace I leave with you, my peace I give unto you,' and He is truth. Not one good word that He has spoken hath failed or shall fail in the last hour. They will say I died of a broken heart, but thou dost know better, my Henri."

"I do, and I will tell the truth," burst impetuously from Henri's lips.

"Nay, my child, I charge thee, as thou lovest me, seal thy lips until thou art safe beyond their power. A word, a look of suspicion, would be thy death-warrant. If thou canst, rejoin thine own people, the fugitives of Carcassone, and may God give thee rest, and deal kindly with thee as thou hast dealt with me."

"Hath my lord no parting word, no message for friend or relative?" asked Henri in a broken voice.

Some thought of long ago stirred the heart of the dying youth, and brought a faint glow to his pale cheek. Yet so long did the silence continue, that the page began to fear his question had been misunderstood. But it was not so. Raymond was wrestling with the last and strongest of earth's passions, and gathering power to put it calmly aside. At length he said, "I have no message, no relative survives who will mourn me. Yet didst thou chance to know, I should be glad to learn aught of my kinsman, the Count of Toulouse."

"Of the Count," returned Henri, "I have heard nothing special, nor yet of his son, but — "

"Well?" said Raymond, observing his hesitation.

"At an inn where I stopped on my way thither, I conversed with a knight who had been in the train of the Lady Beatrice." Raymond heard the name with greater apparent calmness than Henri pronounced it, only a slight quiver passed over his face. "They have brought her to a convent in Spain for safety during these troublous times. The knight said the war and its consequences had affected her deeply."

"She is safe then, and at peace," said Raymond. "In everything God has cared for me. I had once a wild, foolish longing to send a token — "

"My lord, I would cross the world to do your pleasure, only tell me."

"No — no — better as it is. It might wake sad memories, and I would not have one moment's pain given for me. I have done with

Conclusion

these thoughts now. There is One I cannot love too well. I will think of Him."

There was a long silence, then Raymond asked feebly, "Is not the sun setting, Henri?" And in truth the rich red light, which told that the short winter's day had reached its close, stole across the couch, illuminating the form of the dying man and that of the young watcher by his side.

"Let in more light," said Raymond, "I have ever loved the light."

Henri went to the casement, and drew aside a piece of tapestry which partially served as a curtain. A flood of light filled the room immediately, and as the boy looked out on the gorgeous array of gold and purple clouds, he thought of the New Jerusalem, "having the glory of God, and her light like unto a stone most precious, even like a jasper stone, clear as crystal."

He said, returning to the couch, "My dear master will soon behold that land which has no need of the sun to shine in it, for 'the Lamb is the light thereof.' What glory that will be!"

"It may be so," answered Raymond, "but I want no glory, save to see His face. He loves me, He will receive me, that is all I know, and all I need." After a pause he added, "Now I am weary, I long to sleep." In a short time he slept (if indeed it was not rather a sort of stupor than a sleep) while Henri watched and wept silently by him during the long hours of darkness.

The next morning brought the zealous Izarn, eager to try once more the effect of his eloquence. But the ear of Raymond was closed to every voice save one, — that one which said, "Inasmuch as you have done it unto one of the least of these my brethren, you have done it unto Me."

For at midnight there came an angel of the Lord, who opened the prison door and set the captive free. The angel's name was Death.

THE CARPENTER OF NISMES

A Huguenot Story

I

WHO HE WAS

AT THE DARKEST HOUR of a dark night, towards the close of the year 1569, two young men were walking up and down the market-place of Nismes. When the moon, struggling through dense masses of cloud, cast a fitful and occasional gleam on their figures and faces, an observer might have noticed that they contrasted strangely with each other. The dress and bearing of the elder betokened him a gentleman; his features were noble and thoughtful, but careworn, a life of constant peril and suffering had left little to tell of youth on his furrowed brow and wasted cheek. His arm was linked within that of his younger and less dignified companion, whose coarse woolen doublet sufficiently marked his station.

"You are right, monsieur le pasteur," said the peasant youth in tones hoarse with suppressed anguish. "You must leave us. It is written: 'When they persecute you in one city, flee unto another.'"

"Yet it is hard to leave the flock which He has given me, the 'beautiful flock,' in the very mouth of the lion."

Perhaps Emile de Rochet spoke rather to his own heart than to his companion, yet the artisan understood and answered him.

"Can you save them, monsieur, by remaining? Could you save my — my only brother, who perished this day upon yonder spot?" And he pointed to a trampled, blackened spot in the market-place, which the moonbeams at that moment illumined with a cold and ghastly light.

" 'They who have fallen asleep in Christ' have *not* 'perished,' " returned the pastor.

"I know it, monsieur," said the youth, "I know it; how else could I bear to live?" His voice trembled, and his strong frame shook with emotion. After a pause, he resumed more calmly: "It was the Lord's mercy, monsieur le pasteur, that you were not taken when he was. But the good Master knew we could not spare you yet."

"Ill could we spare Jules Maderon," said De Rochet, sadly. "The young, gifted, zealous disciple — he to whose dauntless spirit and strong hand I looked to raise the standard if I fell, or rather when I fell. I have not

Who He Was 87

foregone my trust in the faithfulness of Him who reigns above, but surely His 'way is in the sea, his path in the great waters, and his footsteps are not known.'"

"True, monsieur, true. Only think of it; I was absent at Genlis, working at my trade and fearing no evil, when he went to that assembly and prayed with the poor people. The governor hears of it (alas! that a man whose hairs are white, and who has but a few years more to live, should be so pitiless! — God forgive him!) he sends his spies — Jules is taken; and when I come back he lies fettered in that tower; waiting for his doom. I see him no more until — until this day. I stood close beside him to the last; I told the halberdiers (for I was desperate), that I feared neither the swords they carried nor the fagots they kindled. We clasped each other's hands — I had meant to strengthen him, but I could not say one word. He said to me, 'Good night, brother; we shall meet in the morning of the resurrection.' And so we shall, but the night is a long one, monsieur."

"The day that follows will be glorious, Jacques, and its 'sun shall no more go down.'"

"One thing is strange to me, very strange," resumed the artisan. "Why he was taken — he who could do so much for the cause — gifted as you know he was. He had the good Book all by heart. Never a priest or monk but he could reason down and leave without a word. O monsieur, when he spoke of the blessed Saviour, and what He has done for us, and how good He is, and how loving — it made our hearts burn within us. While I, though his own brother, am a rough, ignorant lad, who never yet could say three words to purpose. I can saw and plane with the best, I know my trade, but, God help me, I know nothing more."

"Yes, my friend, thou dost know one thing more: 'Jesus Christ and Him crucified.'"

"Jesus Christ!" The softened reverent tones in which the youth repeated the Name which is above every name were enough to show how he loved it, and how that love had changed and raised his whole nature. There must have been tears in his eyes, though they were not allowed to fall.

"Monsieur," he said, "I was wild and thoughtless, I cared not for these things. Plenty of food, a dance in the evening with the girls, a game at tennis with the apprenice lads — this was all I wanted. Then *He* came home from his travels, so strangely changed. He talked to me about the Mass, and the Virgin, and the saints; but I could not tell you half he said. At last he would have me go with him to the field-preaching;

and because we were but two, and we so loved each other, I would not say him nay.

"There I heard you preach, monsieur. I forget your words, for it was not your voice I heard, but the voice of One who spake through you, and who said a word to me I never shall forget. That word was, 'Seek My face.' I sought Him; I prayed (mine were poor prayers surely, but the good Lord understands us all). I went again to the field-preaching, and again I heard His voice. This time the words were, 'Thy sins are forgiven thee; go in peace.' Monsieur, do you marvel that my heart is nigh to breaking this hour, because I was not the one to be burned instead of my young brother? Surely the best use the Master could have made of me was to let me die for Him. I can never persuade any one to love Him; but I could have stood firm at the stake, thinking of those blessed words of His; and then Jules might have lived to do such great things for His Name's sake."

"He knows best," returned the pastor. "And thou canst not doubt, Jacques, that He who hath spoken those two words to thee, speaks another also, 'Son, go work today in My vineyard.'"

"*I* work, monsieur? How?"

"With all that you have, which is His, since thou thyself art His."

"Ah, monsieur, I have nothing save my hammer and my plane, my saw with its file, and the power to use them."

"Then use them in His service."

"How so, monsieur?"

"Go and ask Him. This much at least I tell thee, Jacques Maderon, He never yet refused any offering brought by a grateful heart — from the gold, frankincense, and myrrh, spread before Him by the kings of the East to the palm-branches gathered by the feeble hands of the children of Jerusalem."

"I partly understand you, monsieur," said Maderon slowly and thoughtfully. "You mean that I must work well and honestly, and work hard too, that I may have wherewith to help our poor brethren, who are oppressed and plundered by the Governor. One thing I know," he added, "neither Jeannette nor her aged father shall want for bread whilst Jacques Maderon can saw a board in two."

"Jeannette?"

"Ah, monsieur, you did not know then. She and my Jules loved each other from childhood."

De Rochet seemed to shiver with pain, as one might do if a wound were heedlessly touched.

Who He Was

"Are not all these things with Thee, my God?" he said, half aloud. "Dost Thou not mark every cry and tear, and every silent agony? — And the poor girl?" he asked.

Maderon sighed, but answered, "She has her father and her brother." He added after a pause, "The old man is nearly past labour, and Charlot still an apprentice."

Perhaps this was not said without a slight gleam of satisfaction. The only earthly thought, which just then could give Jacques Maderon any feeling akin to pleasure, was his purpose of toiling night and day for those bound to him by the double tie of love to his martyred brother, and faithful service to his Lord and theirs.

"Jacques," said De Rochet, "the hour is late; thou shouldst return to thine home."

"I have no home now, monsieur," replied Maderon. "The spot most like home to me in the whole world is *this*, where I last saw his face. But you, monsieur, have you arranged all things for your escape on the morrow?"

"I have, my friend; or rather, our brethren have arranged for me, and I trust to avoid suspicion. Now, at this midnight hour, a little band await me in the Rue des Carmes, to meet for the last time at our Father's footstool. Wilt thou thither with me?"

"No, monsieur le pasteur, no! Tonight I could not bear the faces of our friends and their questions. With your leave, however, I will walk with you to the gate."

They walked on in silence till they reached the door of a house in the street named by De Rochet.

"Now, farewell, my brother!" said the pastor, extending his hand. "Remember the words our Lord hath said to thee; keep them in thy heart, and live them in thy life, until He says that other word, perchance the best of all, 'Friend, go up higher.'"

"Farewell! God bless and preserve you, Monsieur de Rochet. You have indeed been His messenger to me."

He turned away. The pastor looked after him for a moment, then knocked at the gate — a low peculiar knock. Some one, who was on the watch, admitted him noiselessly and without delay, then closed and bolted the door, leaving Jacques Maderon in the deserted street alone.

II

WHO WERE HIS FRIENDS

THE YEAR in which Jacques Maderon wept his only brother, and Emile de Rochet fled to Genlis to escape the cruelty of the governor of Nismes, was a very dark one in the history of the Huguenots. They had been forced to take up arms in defense, not so much of their liberties as of their very lives; but the God of battles had not, in His mysterious providence, seen fit to give the victory to those who were maintaining His own cause. In the beginning of October the Huguenot army sustained the disastrous defeat of Moncontour, a defeat which nearly struck despair into the steadfast heart of the wise and good Coligny. Amongst the glimpses now and then afforded by history, not only of what men said and did, but of what they really were, few are more touching than that of the retreat from Moncon-

tour. Two princes still in their boyhood —
the Prince of Navarre and the Prince de
Conde — were at this time the nominal chiefs
of the Huguenot army; but the responsibility
devolved, in fact, upon the venerable Admiral. D'Aubigne, the historian of his brother
Huguenots, in his *Histoire Universelle,* thus
depicts at once the weakness and the
strength, the sorrow and the faith, of this
true soldier of the cross. "Surrounded by
weakened towns, terrified garrisons, foreigners without baggage, himself without money,
pursued by an enemy pitiless to all, without
mercy for him, he was abandoned by every
one save by a woman, Queen Jeanne, who
had already reached Niort, to hold out her
hand to the afflicted, and assist in retrieving
their affairs. This old man, consumed by
fever, as they carried him in his litter, lay
revolving all these bitter things, and many
others which were gnawing at his heart, their
sting more grievous than his painful wound,
when L'Estrange, an aged gentleman, and
one of his principal counsellors, travelling
wounded in the same manner, ordered his litter, where the road widened, to be a little
advanced in front of the other, and, putting
forward his head, looked for some time fixedly at his chief. Then the tears filling his eyes,
he turned away with these words, *"Si est ce*

que Dieu est tres doux" (Yet God is a sweet consolation). And so they parted, perfectly understanding each other's thoughts, though quite unable to utter more. But this great captain has been heard to confess to his intimates, that this one little word from a friend sufficed to raise his broken spirits, and restored him to better thoughts of the present, and firm resolutions for the future."

God "who comforteth those that are cast down," was indeed preparing in many ways "a little help" for His tried and suffering servants; and amongst the means by which it was his good pleasure to aid them in their distress, not the least was one resulting from a train of thought which about this time occupied the mind of Maderon, the carpenter of Nismes.

The lonely silent Huguenot artisan steadily pursued his daily toil, working with his hands, not so much to supply his own necessities as those of his friends who were imprisoned or reduced to poverty on account of their steadfast adherence to the truth. He was comforted concerning his brother, for to him, as well as to the great and wise Coligny, God was a sweet consolation. From that lodging in a narrow street many prayers went up which did not fail to reach the ears of the Highest, and such an answer of peace did they bring to the heart of him who prayed, that he soon began again to chant the psalms of Clement Marot while engaged in his work, although when he did so he almost always made choice of the songs of Zion in her days of distress and affliction. Nor was his work itself without a helpful and soothing influence. It was an interesting problem, were any one competent to solve it, to calculate how much sorrow, morbidness, and even despair is put to flight from time to time by hard and continuous toil, still more by such work as requires and repays the exercise of mind.

Jacques Maderon did not forget his self-imposed duty towards the family his martyred brother had loved. He ministered to their wants, read the Book with them in the evenings, when the doors were shut, and exercised a salutary influence over Charlot, a thoughtless though well-disposed and amiable youth.

On his way from their lodging to his own, Maderon always passed near the Porte des Carmes. There was something there which might have attracted the eye of a stranger, though few uneducated men, born and bred upon the spot, would have regarded it with particular interest. The town of Nismes was then and is now supplied with water by means of a Roman aqueduct, which conveys the waters of two springs — the Airon and

Who Were His Friends 97

the Ure — a distance of twenty-five miles, by the celebrated Pont du Gard, to a fountain within the town. Between the Porte des Carmes and the castle, the waters flow through a channel which is closed by a grating.

One evening Maderon looked thoughtfully at this grating as he passed. "I wish those bars were gone," he said to himself, "so could our brethren from Genlis enter unobserved, and take the town for the Princes."

The next evening and the next, the same idea recurred to him, and each time with added force. "I wish *I* could file away those bars," he thought, and the thought went with him to his lonely lodgings, haunted him while he slept, and then mingled with his dreams.

Upon the following evening, Maderon again passed slowly near the Porte des Carmes, thinking this time of the sentinel who stood all night under the castle wall, just above the channel, as if for the express purpose of guarding that one entrance to the strongly fortified town. On this occasion his musings were brought to a close by Jeannette's young brother Charlot, who had been in search of him, and accosted him hastily and with emotion.

"Come home with me, Maderon," he said. "We are in bitter sorrow. Our father — "

"Speak lower, boy," interrupted Maderon. "The passers-by will hear thee. Well?"

"Our father has been seized by the governor's men and thrown into prison."

"Alas, alas!" cried Maderon. "From the governor's prison there is no escape save by denying the faith, and *that* brave old Pierre Mallard will never do."

"I marvel the townsfolk suffer these things," said the youth, "there are so many among them who think with us."

"What of thy sister, Charlot?"

"She weeps — it is well enough for girls and women to weep — but men — "

"I tell thee, lad, be silent till we leave the street. Here we are!"

They had reached the door of the humble dwelling, and were about to climb the steep and narrow stair which led to the room occupied by the Mallards. The sound of a loud, energetic voice struck upon Maderon's ear before the door was opened. A few neighbors who shared the same religious opinions had come in to comfort the afflicted family. When Maderon and Charlot entered, a blacksmith, whose Huguenot leanings were well known, was haranguing the group with the volubility and violent gesticulation so usual amongst his countrymen upon far less exciting occasions.

"We are sheep," he cried, "and like sheep

we are letting ourselves be dragged one by one to the slaughter. Where are the lords, the knights, and the gentlefolk who talked so loudly of the Gospel in the good times, before the Peace was broken, and the country turned into a slaughterhouse? Ah, they are safe enough at Genlis, or elsewhere, little thinking how the yoke presses upon us poor souls. There was our pastor, Monsieur de Rochet — "

"Not a word against the pastor at thy peril, Jean Brusson," interrupted an old man. "He has the heart of a martyr."

"Nor is Jean Brusson the man to deny it," replied the blacksmith. "But this I say, if the exiles of Genlis care for us, let them come back to us like men, and strike one blow for our liberties and lives, trusting us to strike the second. Had I nothing but my hammer, with a strong hand to grasp it, it would do good service against the old tyrant who is starving our brethren in his dungeons, and shedding their blood on his scaffolds. Jacques Maderon, let us hear thy mind on the matter."

Maderon had been listening thoughtfully. "My mind is this, friend Brusson," he answered. "The less said and the more thought and done, the better. Keep thy hammer ready, though, the time may come for thee to use it."

He paused, then added, with some hesitation, "It is written in that Book for which our dear brethren are suffering even unto death, 'Vengeance is mine, I will repay, saith the Lord.' If we strike for vengeance, with wrath and bitter hatred in our hearts, the good Lord will not give us the victory. But it may be that if we ask Him He will have mercy on us, and show us some way to save alive a remnant of His little flock in this great wicked cruel city."

Having said this, he crossed the room, and spoke to the weeping Jeannette and two or three women who were with her. The girl's tears ceased to flow, and she looked up with interest as he told her that he had found means before this to visit his Huguenot brethren confined in the town prison, and to supply them with food and other necessaries, and he would not fail to do as much for his faithful friend, Pierre Mallard.

"Can you take me to see him?" asked Jeannette.

"Perhaps so," returned Jacques, and he stooped down, and added very low, "It may be God will give him back to thee ere long. Good night, my girl." He then gave some directions to Charlot, passed out of the room and went quietly home.

III

THE USE OF A FILE

"CHARLOT," said Maderon, as the youth entered his workshop by appointment on the evening of the day after Pierre Mallard's arrest, "wilt thou aid me to save thy father's life?"

"Try me, friend Jacques," was the eager reply.

"I would have thee count the cost," returned Maderon; "dost thou fear to peril thine own?"

"Not in such a cause," said Charlot.

"Canst thou bear fatigue, and cold, and long watching? Canst thou *wait* as well as work, Charlot?"

"If I know myself, I can."

Maderon looked at him earnestly for some moments.

"One question more," he said at length. "Canst thou keep silence — such silence as the dead keep in their graves — until I bid thee speak?"

"Shall I swear it?"

"Promise rather — God hears every word."

"I promise, as I stand in His presence."

"Good, now go back to thy sister. Tell her I want thee for some work, and as we must labor late, thou shalt stay the night with me. Say I will pay thy time, and thou mayest bring food and wine to the father tomorrow. Take thy cloak and return as quickly as thou canst."

Charlot did as he was directed. When he returned Maderon stood before him, equipped in his coarsest and strongest doublet. He looked pale, but there was an expression of quiet determination in his face; something that told of courage to do, to dare, and to endure. With just such a look he would have mounted the scaffold or clasped the stake, and he would have done so with just as little consciousness that he was performing any but the most ordinary Christian duty.

"With the good help of God," he said, "I am going to file the bars of the grating in the channel at the Porte des Carmes, that our brethren from Genlis may enter to take the town, and to deliver thy father and all the other Huguenots in this oppressed city."

Charlot gazed at him, speechless with astonishment. At last he said, "Who put thee

The Use of A File 103

upon this business? Who counselled thee, bade thee do it?"

"God," said Maderon reverently.

"What dost thou mean?" asked Charlot, awed by the solemnity of his manner.

"That I believe and am sure He wills me to do this work, and that He will aid me to accomplish it."

"But," said Charlot, "the sentinel who stands by the castle, wilt thou work under his very eyes?"

"I have considered all," replied Maderon. "The sentinel is changed every hour. He rings a bell when his time has expired, and before his place is taken by a comrade there is an interval in which a man might count three, four, or even five hundred. Those are the precious moments God gives me to do my work in. See" — he raised his doublet and showed Mallard a cord which he had wound many times round his waist, — "I will lie in the ditch, and thou must stand by the wall in a dark, safe place I have discovered, holding the end of this cord (it is long enough); when the bell rings and the soldier leaves his post, thou shalt pull it, and that will be my signal to work as if for life; when the soldier returns, another pull, and I lie safe and quiet until the next hour gives me my chance again. So on until the morning light."

"Maderon, the work will take us a year."

"It will not," returned Maderon quietly, "nor even a month."

" 'Twill be freezing work too in that ditch these winter nights."

"Better I should freeze than thy father should burn."

"If the sound of thy file should betray thee?" suggested Charlot.

"The rushing of the water will drown it; and lest the light should discover what is done in the darkness (though it be no deed of darkness), I will hide the traces of my work every morning with mud and wax. Charlot, dost thou hesitate? Wilt thou make me repent that I have chosen to aid me in this deed, in preference to any man in Nismes, a lad who has his father to save from the burning pile, or the slow death in prison, which is worse?"

"No, Jacques, no! I will stand beside thee to the last, God helping me."

"God help us both, and establish the work of our hands upon us." Maderon took a file from among his tools, saying as he did so, "The Lord hath need of thee. Monsieur de Rochet was right. Come, Charlot, every moment is precious."

The two young men went out together, and that night they began their work.

IV

A PRISON SCENE

IN ONE OF THE GLOOMIEST CELLS of the gloomy town prison of Nismes, Pierre Mallard lay on his straw pallet, heavily ironed. His frame was wasting under the influence of the prison fever, the pestilence that walked in the darkness of those abodes of misery, piercing with its subtle shafts many an unknown and unnoticed victim. In those evil days Christ had His martyrs in the dungeon as well as on the scaffold and at the stake. Nor were all so fortunate as Mallard. It was evident from a few simple comforts and even luxuries which the cell contained that friends had been permitted to visit him and to minister to his wants. No day, however, since his imprisonment had been so marked with white as this, the fourteenth since those gloomy gates had closed upon him. He heard the key grate heavily in the door, which was then swung open by the rough though not unfeeling prison official as he ushered in a young girl, closely veiled, and with a basket on her arm.

"Prisoner Mallard, thy daughter has come to see thee."

In a moment father and child were locked in each other's arms, with emotions those alone can understand in whose hearts sorrow has deepened everything, even the capacity to enjoy.

Mallard was the first to speak. "So thou hast come to me, *thou!* How didst thou gain admission?"

"Jacques is acquainted with the second jailer; he managed all, he is good to us, my father."

"There are many good to us, my child, and One above them all who hears the sighing of His prisoners."

Jeannette could not help mentally concluding the passage, — "With the greatness of thy power preserve thou those that are appointed to die," and the words became a passionate prayer, a wild, bitter cry for help, almost ending in tears. So sadly changed was the dear face on which she looked, "appointed to die" seemed indeed to be written there.

She said as calmly as she could whilst she

A Prison Scene

caressed the hand she held, "My dear father is ill."

"Not very ill, my child. I have no pain, I am only weak and weary. It refreshes me to see thee; thy face is more to me than sunshine, and so it has ever been."

"But not like the sunshine, Father," said Jeannette, "not at least of late — too often dim with tears. Ah, I was ungrateful to weep the past so bitterly, whilst *thou* wert left with me. If the good God will only give thee back to us, no more vain tears shall fall, it shall be all thankfulness, even in this poor heart of mine."

"Child, our Father knows our frame, and, I doubt not, will sometimes be tenderer to us than we are to ourselves. It is not said 'sorrow not,' only not 'without hope.' But our time is short; tell me of thyself, of Charlot."

"We have lacked nothing, Father," she answered in a trembling voice. "Yet do not think we are leaning altogether on our kind friends. Charlot works hard after hours with Jacques Maderon, with whom, indeed, he stays the night, that he may not go to and fro at unseasonable hours."

"Poor boy! he must not work too hard."

"It is his pleasure, my father, to work for thee, and for me also. See, he hath sent thee this," and she took a flask of wine from her little basket.

"Would I could share it with some of my poor brethren who are not so well provided," said Mallard.

"I have more to tell thee of Charlot," Jeannette resumed. "God ofttimes gives great comfort where He sends great trouble. My father, Charlot is changed."

Mallard's eye brightened; he half raised himself, and looked eagerly at his daughter.

"None would know the wild thoughtless lad, who gave thee so many anxious hours by joining the foolish frolics of his brother apprentices. It would seem as if, in leaving us, thou hadst left thy spirit behind with him. He is tender, thoughtful, serious, and depressed, as I doubt not with anxious thoughts of thee, perhaps also of himself. Last night he said to me, 'Sister, pray for me; I have more need for prayer than thou canst know.'"

"Now God be praised!" said the old man, while tears of grateful joy filled his eyes, "I knew He would hear my prayer. Jeannette, if He should in His love and mercy call me home by this quiet path, by a death which is not like other deaths thou hast known of — Nay, do not shudder, do not weep. *His* death was glorious, my child, the greatest glory man can have on this poor earth, — greater perhaps than the bright angels have, who behold the Father's face. Only I am so

A PRISON SCENE 109

weak, too weak, I fear, to be a blessed martyr like him thou mournest; therefore, I will thank my Saviour if He sends His messenger some day or night to this lonely room, and calls me out of the darkness into His presence, where there is light and joy."

"Do not speak so, my father," said Jeannette through her tears. "There is hope of deliverance."

"What hope, my poor child? I would not sadden thee with needless fears, but neither would I have thee stay thy heart upon false hopes. Without denying his faith, no Huguenot leaves this prison save for the marketplace."

"There *is* hope," said Jeannette earnestly. "I can scarcely tell from whence the light comes, but I see it. Charlot hopes. Sometimes he drops dark hints of deliverance possible — near. He said yester eve, 'When my father comes home, I will tell him why I go no more to the tennis court.' I answered, 'Alas, brother, *when?*' He said, donning his cloak and his beret, 'Thou shalt know a week hence.' And sometimes — But hark, the jailer returns. Can it be that the time has passed?"

It was true. The father and child were forced to part, neither knowing whether another meeting would be theirs on this side of the grave. Still they were both calm, at least in outward appearance, as they committed each other to the love and care of their heavenly Protector.

And yet, notwithstanding the hopefulness with which she spoke, the heart of Jeannette was very sorrowful when she saw the prison-gate closed, and went her way homeward. Her father's words of mournful resignation echoed in her ears and lingered in her heart. She did not think, as the happy sometimes do, that death was a strange impossible thing, which should not and could not invade the charmed circle of her loved ones. He who had been dearest to her upon earth "was not," and death, when it has once drawn near to deep natures, stands close at hand for evermore. The same stroke that bids them mourn for one bids them tremble for all the rest.

A fortnight had passed away, and still Maderon toiled on with untiring perseverance. Every morning found him half frozen with cold and worn out with fatigue, but rejoicing in the progress made during the few precious moments in which he was permitted to work. He was cheerful and hopeful, scarcely once, from the commencement of his arduous undertaking until its conclusion, doubting its final accomplishment. Perhaps the secret of his success lay in the use made of the long idle hours as much as in the brief intervals during which he employed his file.

In those hours his work was prayer, and no work is half so rich in results. He sometimes feared lest the long watching might prove too severe a trial for his youthful companion, and injure a frame which had not yet attained the full strength of manhood. Under this apprehension he proposed to Charlot that they should confide their secret to another friend, who might take his turn at the place of watching.

" 'Twere a strange way to serve thy father," he said, "were I to deprive him of an only son."

"Never fear for me, Jacques," replied the youth. "I am able for my work, which, besides, is nothing to thine," he added, "and I really love my place beneath the wall. I have *thought* more there than elsewhere in all my life."

"Courage then," replied Maderon, "courage and patience. The work is almost forward enough to give our friends a word of warning."

And after fifteen nights of labor, mysterious rumors of deliverance at hand were spread abroad amongst the Huguenots of Nismes; while Jacques Maderon departed early in the morning for Genlis, taking with him his tools, that the uninitiated might suppose his object was merely to seek for work.

V

CONCLUSION

IN A LITTLE "TEMPLE" at Genlis, Emile de Rochet was expounding the Scriptures to a congregation chiefly composed of refugees from Nismes, when Maderon entered silently, and took his place upon a bench amongst the listeners. The pastor's quick eye marked and recognized him immediately, and the thought passed through his mind that he too had been forced by persecution to flee from his native city. As soon, therefore, as his discourse was concluded, and before his hearers were dispersed, he summoned the carpenter to his side, feeling sure that all the refugees would listen with interest to the tidings brought by their humble fellow-townsman.

Every eye fixed on Maderon as he walked quickly through the room and took his place beside De Rochet. Having grasped his extended hand and wrung it warmly, he looked around on the little assembly in which were many faces that he knew.

"My brethren," he said, and he spoke very calmly, without hesitation or embarrassment, "come with me to Nismes. God has given the city into our hands."

"Art thou mad, or dreaming, Jacques Maderon?" cried one voice and another from amongst the listeners.

"I am neither," replied Maderon. "Listen to me. I have filed the bars of the grating which closes the channel at the Porte des Carmes, and any man of you who chooses may enter Nismes this night."

"Impossible! He is a spy, traitor! It is some snare!" Such exclamations as these, from different parts of the room, evinced the difficulty which the refugees not unnaturally felt in accepting a statement, so improbable in itself, from the lips of a humble artisan.

It had not occurred to Maderon that they would doubt his word, or hesitate to engage in the enterprise to which he summoned them. A look of grief and disappointment passed across his face, and he said simply, but with intense earnestness, "My brethren, your friends are dying every day in the governor's dungeons. They call upon you to deliver them, and upon your heads their blood will rest if you refuse to obey the call."

He paused, then added, with an appealing

glance at De Rochet, "Monsieur le pasteur, tell them that I speak the truth."

Then De Rochet spoke out, his clear deep voice stilling every murmur in the assembly. "I would stake my life, and every other life I prize, upon the truth of Maderon's words. To prove what I say, I go back with him this hour to Nismes. Who volunteers to accompany us?"

"God bless you, monsieur!" cried Maderon.

"Well, monsieur le pasteur," said a young Huguenot gentleman in the assembly, "if you will risk your neck upon this errand, it shall never be said that we of the sword and hauberk proved less daring than a man of peace."

And a stout tradesman added, "If your jewelled broadsword lead the way, chevalier, I have a good cutlass in a strong hand to follow you."

Stimulated by the example and influence of the pastor and the chevalier, one and another and another volunteered, until a little band was formed, which De Rochet and Maderon judged sufficient for the enterprise.

A very brief preparation sufficed them, and after a short but most fervent prayer for their success, offered by the pastor, they began their march, while the shades of evening darkened over Genlis. The weather was settled, and seemed to afford them the prospect

Conclusion 115

of a night calm and fine, yet sufficiently dark to favor their enterprise.

"Now, carpenter," said the chevalier to Maderon, "should we find that thou hast led us into a snare, 'twill fare ill with thee."

"First take Nismes, monsieur le chevalier," replied Maderon, "then do what you wilt with me."

"Look! See! What was that?" cried the Huguenots, standing still and gazing at each other with pale, agitated faces.

A vivid flash of lightning, followed by a heavy peal of thunder, was the cause of their alarm. This sudden frown of nature, coming as it did where all had seemed but a few moments before so calm and untroubled, brought dismay into hearts not emancipated from the childish superstitions of the age. Nor were all the little band of such resolute temper as De Rochet and Maderon.

Startled and terrified, they crowded together like a flock of sheep, and seemed disposed to turn their faces again in the direction of Genlis. But De Rochet raised his voice once more to animate them.

"Courage, my brethren!" he cried; "the lightning shows that God Himself will fight for us." And throwing himself into the midst of the wavering group, he besought them earnestly, and with impassioned gestures, to persevere in the good work they had undertaken, and not to doubt the presence and assistance of Him whose cause they were maintaining.

Meanwhile the Catholics of Nismes had retired to rest, little anticipating any disturbance of their quiet slumbers. Not so the persecuted Huguenots. Under the direction of Maderon, Charlot Mallard had hinted to many of them that they should hold themselves in readiness. Between the night and the morning a cry was raised, which the silent, anxious watchers recognized as the expected signal. They seized whatever weapons came first to hand, and rushed eagerly from their houses to the scene of action. Only about twenty of the exiles from Genlis entered by the way so strangely opened by Maderon; and by this little band the Huguenots of Nismes were not so much delivered from their oppressors as given courage to effect their own deliverance. The Catholics, astonished and terrified, had few means of resistance at hand; the Huguenots were numerous, and fighting for faith, and freedom, and even for life; and after a short, sharp, confused struggle in the streets, the town was theirs.

Jean Brusson did good service with his hammer in the melee, and better still in the prison, whither the victorious Huguenots

Conclusion

rushed, eager to taste the sweetest fruit of victory, the joy of delivering their captive brethren. Brusson, performed, with noisy glee, the agreeable task of freeing them from their fetters; while Maderon, with deeper and less demonstrative joy, found his way to the prison of Mallard, accompanied by Charlot.

It took some time to make the old man believe that the city was in the hands of his brethren, and that he was safe and free. When at last he did so, tears of grateful joy came more readily to his eyes than words to his lips. So deeply was he moved, that Maderon thought it wisest to defer one of the best parts of his communication, the tidings that his beloved Charlot had been greatly instrumental in bringing about this happy result. He soon found that Mallard longed for his home, for the close room in a narrow street was as truly home to him as if it had been a chalet amidst the snow-clad Alps. He contrived, therefore, a crude litter with the aid of the willing, happy Charlot, and in a short time the old man was lying on his own bed, tended lovingly by Jeannette.

The young girl busied herself in little tender cares for his comfort, scarcely daring to indulge in a moment's retrospective thought, lest she should be rendered incapable of action. She was very thankful; from that day and hour a subdued and quiet trustfulness, that was almost happiness, began to take the place of mournful dreams of the past, and gloomy anticipations of the future. Never again did that blackness of darkness return upon her soul, which, in those first days after the martyrdom of Jules Maderon, had seemed to veil both earth and heaven from her sight. God had set His bow in the cloud that overshadowed her; He had shown her a token not to be mistaken, of His watchful care and tender love; and that love, which includes within itself the promise and the essence of all good, she would never afterwards permit herself to doubt.

"What am I, an empty talker, beside this great doer?" said Martin Luther, when he heard of the victorious faith and heroic fortitude of an obscure martyr. A similar thought filled the mind of De Rochet, as he entered Maderon's workshop towards the close of the following day. Perhaps, unconsciously to himself, he expected some change in the appearance, speech, and conduct of the man, corresponding to the strange revolution which had transformed the humble mechanic into a hero. If so, he was disappointed. The carpenter was seated at his bench, engaged upon a rather elaborate piece of work, and as truly "a whole man" to that "one thing," as if he had no thought or aspiration beyond.

Conclusion

De Rochet laid his hand on his shoulder, "What, my friend, at work today?" he said.

Maderon rose quickly, and saluted the pastor as usual, with respect and cordiality.

"My work would not wait, monsieur," he said. "I have promised it tomorrow; and moreover, a little extra pains may not be amiss. I would have these Catholic gentlemen say, 'Huguenot tradesmen are always the best.'"

"Faithful in the least, faithful also in much," thought De Rochet, and he could not help adding aloud, "Show me the man who performs every little daily task as unto the Lord, and I will show you one who will not fail when called to do or to suffer greatly for His sake. Maderon, thou hast fulfilled nobly the charge I gave thee that night in the market-place."

Maderon replied with a frank simplicity in which there was no mixture of pride or self-consciousness. "And I have found, monsieur, that the Master needed me, Jacques Maderon the carpenter, just as I was; and since I had only my hands to serve Him with, He had a work for my hands to do. But, monsieur, what of the castle? the Catholics hold that still."

"They cannot continue to hold it more than a few days. A messenger has been dispatched this morning to inform the Princes and the Admiral that the town is theirs. 'Twill be happy tidings to them, and to all who have the good cause at heart."

"True, monsieur; but the Lord's great mercy has done most of all for us, the poor Huguenots of Nismes, who may now lie down to sleep at night and go to our work by day in peace and safety, none making us afraid." He added with a thoughtful, half-doubting glance at De Rochet, "Is it possible — think you — that — that — my brother Jules may know of these things?"

"I dare not say so, Jacques; there are passages in Scripture which would seem to intimate the contrary. But what matters it? We are quite sure that he knows the end, that he rests in the full certainty that truth and right will triumph at last. Why then should we care that he should know every little step of the way?"

"You are right, monsieur, only I would have liked — " his lip trembled, and he turned his face away for a moment. Then he resumed calmly, "I see that the same Lord who wanted him in His bright home above, wanted me in this poor workshop here. Doubtless, when my work is done, He will call me also to Himself. Meanwhile I will work on hopefully and happily, knowing that each day's toil is done unto Him, as truly as it was for His sake I filed the grating at the Port des Carmes."

A CHILD'S VICTORY

I

THE SHADOW OF DEATH

On a sultry summer's day, seven hundred years ago, a little girl stood at a street door in one of the close, narrow alleys of a Flemish town. Her dress indicated poverty, though not neglect.

Other children were playing near. She heard their voices, and looked at them for a few moments with curiosity and interest in her large blue eyes, but apparently she had no wish to join their sports.

Far more earnestly she gazed to the right, where the long alley terminated in a broader street, where a stream of intense vivid sunlight illuminated a corner of the shaded alley, with a Madonna in her niche, as well as the quaint carvings that adorned the house of rich Messer Andreas the weaver. What would little Arlette have given to see one figure that she knew turn from the sunshine into the shadow! Young as she was, she had already learned one of woman's saddest lessons — *watching*.

"Child, where art thou?" moaned a faint voice from within the house.

In another instant she stood by the bedside of her dying mother. All too surely had Death, that great king, sealed those wasted features with his own signet, that the purpose might not be changed concerning her.

Yet, to judge by the calm that overspread them, he was in this instance no king of terrors — no king, but a servant rather, a herald of the "King immortal, invisible," sent from His presence to summon one of His children home.

"Thou seest no one, child?"

"No, Mother. Tomorrow — perhaps tomorrow he will come."

But the child's faith in tomorrow failed to communicate itself to the dying woman.

"No one," she continued, without heeding the words of Arlette, "no one, — and it is well. Though long and sore has been the conflict, I can now say it is well. My child, when *he* comes, tell him we shall meet above; — tell him that I waited — waited just to look in his face once more, and to say good-by; but now the call has come, and I must go. As for thee — "

She paused, and a look of exhaustion

passed over her face. The little girl did not weep but maintained the quiet self-possession of an older person.

"Arlette, I must ask thee a hard thing. Wilt thou do it for me?" She raised herself slightly, and fixed her dark eyes earnestly on the sorrowing child.

"Mother, I will do anything — anything!"

"My child, listen to me. Look in my face, and tell me that if I grow worse, as it must be, thou wilt not fear."

"Fear what, Mother?"

"Fear to stand thus beside me quite alone — thy hand in mine — none other with us save the great God above who is with us always."

Arlette did not speak. Her face was very pale and her lips were compressed.

"Promise me, child of my heart, promise me that happen what may, thou wilt call no one, bring no one here."

Arlette looked up quickly. "Save our good neighbor, the Vrow Cristine, who hath been so kind and helpful to us?"

"No, child, not even Cristine. Thou canst not understand. And yet perchance thou canst, for sorrow hath been thy teacher, and she teaches well and quickly. If Cristine comes to sit beside me when I lie senseless she will say within herself, 'Now I can fetch the priest and make all right for my poor neighbor. And he will come and pray his blasphemous prayers and pour his useless oil upon my brow. Then, Arlette, we shall have touched the accursed thing, and when thy father knows it, it will break his heart."

Arlette did not answer immediately. She stood pale and motionless, her eyes fixed on her mother's face. At last she said in a low resolved tone, "That shall never be, Mother."

And as she spoke, the self-command so unnatural for her years gave way, and with true childlike sorrow she wept and wailed, "Mother! Mother!"

"Poor child, poor little one," said the mother soothingly.

The child soon conquered her tears and sobs, and sat down quietly in the dark corner beside her mother's couch. But her frame still quivered with suppressed emotion. What a long, long day it was, and how unlike any other day in her brief experience of life!

Her mother slumbered uneasily from time to time, and would then talk of strange things that she could not understand, sometimes speaking to the absent father as if he were near her, and again wailing feebly that he would not come. But happily for Arlette, these wanderings, which filled her with terror, did not continue. As evening drew on, the dying woman lay calm and still. At last

THE SHADOW OF DEATH 127

sleep came, not like the feverish slumbers of the day, but quiet and restful, "as if upon the spirit worn distilled some healing balm."

The little watcher kept her place, from which, for some hours, she had only moved to smooth her mother's pillow or to bring a cooling drink to her lips. And now she feared to disturb her by a motion or a breath.

The kind-hearted Cristine, wife of their neighbor the fuller, came to the door with inquiries, which Arlette answered in a low voice.

"She sleeps, sayest thou?" said the hearty, good-natured Vrow in a tolerably loud whisper, and pushing the door a little more open. "Poor child, art thou not lonely and afraid? Let me come in and sit with thee awhile."

In her heart Arlette longed to accept the proffered companionship, but mindful of her promise she declined it firmly though gratefully.

"Is there nought I can do for thee? Wouldst thou not have me call the leech? He is a good man and right friendly to the poor. Bless thee, child, if thy mother feared to summon him because she had little to give, Messer Franz would rather leave a mark behind him with such as thou than take it from thee."

"He hath been here," returned Arlette sadly. "He came this morning, and said there was nothing more that he could do now."

"Ah, I see." As softly as she could the good woman stepped into the room. When she beheld the white, still face on the pillow, the expression of her own changed, and she sighed and shook her head. She spoke again to Arlette, but without looking at her. "My little one, it were well, methinks, to fetch the holy father, that he may pray beside her, and do what is right for her poor soul. There, there," seeing that the child looked pale and frightened, "I did not mean to grieve thee; but we must think of the soul that has to live for ever."

"My father is coming home," said the child timidly. "We must wait for him."

"Thy father!" repeated Vrow Cristine in some surprise. "God grant he may come, but, my poor child — "

"There is one nigh that wilt not wait for him," she was about to add, but unwillingness to terrify Arlette kept her silent.

After making her promise to call her if she needed help, she withdrew to consult with her husband whether they might not take her to their own home, when a few short hours had made her an orphan.

Meanwhile the light of the long summer day began to fade, and in the dusk Arlette trembled with vague terror. All the familiar

THE SHADOW OF DEATH

objects in the little room looked strange and ghastly in the uncertain twilight. When she turned from them to gaze at the dear face on the pillow, gleaming white through the darkness, that too seemed changed. Was it indeed her mother — her own mother, that she loved, and from whom she had never been separated? Would she not speak to her, look at her again? Was she — she could not for worlds have uttered the word that was in her thoughts. Her heart almost stood still in its terror. She bowed her head and hid her face in the coverlet, not only in sorrow, but in fear — an awful fear that seemed to oppress her like a heavy weight, and stifled a cry that had almost passed her lips unawares.

Beyond utterance was the sense of relief with which she heard footsteps, supposing the kind Vrow Cristine was coming once more to offer help and companionship. Surely, just for a little while, she might let her stay.

"But no," she thought immediately, "it is a man's footstep — perhaps it is the fuller, Cristine's husband." Any one would have been welcome now, any one save perhaps a dark-robed priest.

It was neither priest nor fuller nor physician. A few hasty strides brought into the room a tall gaunt man, long robed, wearing wooden sandals, to whose arms Arlette sprang with a passionate cry, "My father!"

II

THE VOICE OF THE PAST

ON THE EVENING OF THE NEXT DAY, Robert the Wanderer (for such was the name by which Arlette's father was generally known), sat in that little room, as silent and nearly as motionless as the form that lay, draped in spotless white, on the couch before him. His eye might have rested at the same moment upon the treasure God had recalled and the treasure He had still left him; for Arlette, worn out by watching and by tears, had sunk to sleep beside her mother, the warm cheek of the living almost touching the cold features of the dead.

Robert did look on her long and thoughtfully; in mourning for the dead he mourned also for the living. Bitter self-reproach mingled with his sorrow. There was some ground for the feeling, though not so much as in the anguish of his first hour of bereavement he fancied.

Robert the Wanderer was the son of a prosperous tradesman of Ghent. His father destined him for the Church, and being naturally studious and thoughtful he gladly acquiesced in the plan. He had nearly completed the necessary course of preparation, when he formed the acquaintance of a stranger from southern Germany, an earnest, eloquent man, resembling in his dress a wandering monk, yet with some differences, in his manners simple, austere and grave, and speaking of invisible realities as one who had felt their power.

With this friend (who in truth belonged to the sect then called the *Cathari*), young Robert held long conferences, and finally borrowed from him his most precious treasure, a manuscript copy of the Gospels, which he usually kept concealed beneath his robe of dark serge. In his lonely chamber the student perused this volume, and often he wept and prayed over its contents in sorrowful perplexity until the night was far advanced. For all the ideas of his childhood and youth had received a mighty shock. From the conversations of his friend and the lessons of his book he began to suspect that the vast superstructure which he called "the Church" was built upon a shifting foundation of sand.

God gave him courage and honesty (it was no small gift) not at this point to close the book and to stifle the misgivings that tortured his soul, but rather steadfastly to resolve that he would sift the matter to the bottom, that he would follow on to know the truth and then abide in it. Thus the distinguishing tenets of Romanism — purgatory, penance, image-worship, invocation of saints, justification by works — were one by one loosened and cast off from his spirit, "like worn-out fetters."

But then arose the question, So much cast away, what should he retain as truth? Was all faith superstition? Was certainty impossible to man? Was he indeed doomed to doubt and perplexity, or might he somewhere discover a "great rock foundation," upon which he might safely build his hopes of immortality?

It has been said that, "when the mortal, in the moment between his first sigh and his last smile, between the lightning of life and the thunder of death, finds his Christ, he is already at the goal and has lived enough." Some such feeling filled the soul of Robert, when he found in the person of Christ all that his nature needed — truth to satisfy his intellect, love to fill his heart.

He accepted Christ as his Saviour, his Guide and his Teacher, relying on the promise, "He that followeth me shall not walk in darkness, but shall have the light of life"; thus following, he was taught to choose the good and to refuse the evil, good meaning with him that which sprang from Christ as its center and led to Him as its end, and evil being all that came from self or terminated in self. His friend aided him by his counsels and his prayers, and rejoiced with him when he found light and peace.

"And now," he said, as Robert joyfully confessed his faith, "what wilt thou do, my friend?"

The young disciple was not prepared with an answer to this inquiry. It had not indeed occurred to him that any particular course of action was a necessary consequence of his change. But as he pondered, he felt that it would now be impossible for him to live as he would otherwise have done, and that he must choose his part, or else prove a traitor to Him whom he loved and desired to serve.

Kneeling in his chamber, he prayed, "Lord, what wilt Thou have me to do?" Events, which Pascal calls "masters sent to us from the hand of God," answered the question for him.

His absence from the rites of the Church brought him under suspicion. He was questioned by his family, and felt himself obliged to avow his faith. "Heresy" was then a new and strange phenomenon to the good people of Ghent, but they regarded it with vague horror. To save his life, the suspected one was forced to fly. In company with his friend, the German missionary, Robert quit his native city for ever, and determined to devote the remainder of his life to the task of imparting the truths he had found so precious.

"As a son with a father," he labored with his aged companion in the gospel, passing from town to town and from village to village sowing the good seed "here a little and there a little."

After some years he chanced to become acquainted at Bruges with a man who proved to be a native of his own city, and also a fellow-craftsman and friend of his father's. While traveling homewards with his family, this man had been detained at Bruges by an infectious fever, one of those pestilences which so often walked on their silent deadly way through the ill-cleansed and ill-ventilated alleys of the medieval cities. His wife and two sons fell victims to the disorder, and not long afterwards the broken-hearted father followed them to the grave, not, however, until through the teaching of Robert he was enabled to rejoice in a hope full of immortality.

A fair and gentle girl was thus left the sole survivor of the family. Friendless and unprotected in a strange city, what could she do but weep and pray that if the prayer were not a sinful one, she might soon be permitted to rejoin her parents? She had some relatives in Ghent, but the short journey was then more formidable, more impracticable for a lonely girl than a voyage to the ends of the earth would be in the present day.

Robert showed unwearied kindness and sought in every way to aid and comfort her and from the compassion that prompted these efforts the transition to a different sentiment is proverbially easy. He might, if he had so desired, have found means to send her safely to her friends in Ghent, but another course of action occurred to his mind, which he so far preferred that he found no difficulty in persuading himself that he ought to adopt it. No vow bound him. The laws of Rome forbidding marriage he regarded as vain traditions of men, and considered the strongest ties of human affection by no means inconsistent with his calling as a laborer in the vineyard of the Lord.

Robert, the wanderer and the outcast, who knew not and must never know the true meaning of the word home, needed no other commentary upon the declaration, "such shall have trouble in the flesh," than that supplied by the short sad life of her who lay before him in her shroud. The missionary's wife had been happier even in distress and danger, in manifold perplexities and anxieties, than had she possessed all the wealth and enjoyment that earth could give. Sometimes, when his heart was cast down within him, he had been told so with loving words and looks, of which the remembrance almost brought a tear to his burning eyelids.

At another hour he would feel and understand that this was indeed but the simple truth, but now his heart was too sorrowful to be just to itself. Forgetting the joy they two had had together, and even the blessed knowledge he had been privileged to impart to his beloved one, he only remembered the perils into which he had drawn her, and the many cares she had endured for him, which perchance had shortened as well as embittered her life.

And the living link that still remained between him and the dead, his child — his precious beautiful child — as he gazed on her sleeping form his trouble "did not pass but grew," the clouds of sorrow waxed darker and darker around him. Arlette, the missionary's child, was not wanted in the world! Well would it be if she joined her mother in that home where there are "many mansions," for elsewhere there seemed to be no place for her.

The kind Vrow Cristine, when she came

into the darkened room that morning to perform the last sad offices for the departed, had indeed more than hinted that the child was welcome to share the home and the bread of her little ones as long as her father wished; but how could he consent to this? How could he surrender her to the care of those who professed a soul-destroying faith, of those whose mistaken kindness would lead them to induce her to submit to influences which he regarded with abhorrence the most intense? Rather a thousand times would he see her laid in the grave beside her mother than thus peril the interests of her immortal soul. Another alternative remained. He considered it long and anxiously, and finally resolved that, with God's good help, he would embrace it.

"Arlette, my child, awake; thou hast slumbered long enough."

The little sleeper started, and looked up; it was her father's voice that spoke, and her father's form that bent lovingly over her. Her first sensation was one of joy at his return.

"Yes," she thought, "he is here indeed, the long-watched-for, the beloved; he will not leave us again, we are safe now in his care — *We!*"—

In a moment all the anguish of the past came over her, and she knew too surely that her mother was no more.

The Voice of the Past

"Mother! Mother!" she cried from the depths of her heart. Weeping, sobbing, shivering, she threw herself upon the dead. Tenderly and silently her father raised her, clasped her in his strong arms and held her close to his heart. There at last the passion of her grief spent itself, and she grew calm, though almost exhausted. She began to observe his dress, the room, the shadows on the wall, and in a weary half listless way to wonder why he did not weep too. With an effort she raised herself a little, and looked up in his face. It was white and rigid, and terrible as the face of one who has seen a horror he can never reveal and never forget.

As he spoke to her, and in a low quiet voice, the dread she felt vanished quite away before the dear familiar tones, which seemed gentler than ever. He said, "By-and-by I will bring thee to thy friend Vrow Cristine. Thou shalt stay with her to-night."

"Why so, Father? I would rather stay with thee."

"Not now, my child. I have — I have work to do." The words were spoken with an evident effort, and the strong man trembled.

"Bid farewell to Cristine and to thy little playfellows, Arlette, for tomorrow thou shalt go hence with me."

She looked up with surprise and interest.

"Yes, my poor child. God has left us two

alone in the world, and with His good help nothing but death shall part us."

"And wilt thou take me with thee to the strange lands where thou goest, my father?"

"Even so. It will be a rough uncertain life for such as thou, but if love and care can make it easy to thee, God knows they shall not fail. Thou art my sole treasure now." A burning tear fell on the child's forehead. With a child's art she answered by a kiss. Carefully instructed in the Scriptures, it was not unnatural that the story of Ruth should occur to her at the moment.

"I will be thy Ruth to thee, Father," she said softly. " 'Where thou goest, I will go; where thou lodgest, I will lodge.' "

"And thy father's God shall be thine, my precious child."

"There is more in the verse, Father. Let me say it all. 'Where thou diest, I will die, and there will I be buried.' "

"God forbid!" escaped almost involuntarily from the lips of Robert. But he added a moment afterwards, "Yet His will be done. He knoweth what is best for thee and me."

After a short interval the good-natured face of Cristine appeared at the door. "So please you, neighbor, I have come for the child," she said, "and my husband hath summoned thy friend as thou desiredst. He will be here soon."

The Voice of the Past   141

"God reward thee, my kind friend," replied Robert heartily, as he took her hand.

The good woman hesitated for a moment, and then said in a tone of mild, almost deferential expostulation, "I know well, Master Robert, that thou art a wise man, and I am only a simple woman. Still the neighbors will talk amongst themselves even if I keep silence, and in good sooth, master, 'twould be hard to disprove what they whisper, when never a priest —"

"No more of this *now*, good Cristine, as thou pitiest my sorrow," Robert interrupted. "But ere I leave this place, for leave it I must tomorrow, if I may, I would talk for an hour with thee and thy husband."

"And right welcome, neighbor. Now, my pretty one, come with me. The children have wanted thee all day."

"Father, dear Father," whispered Arlette, "may I not stay?"

"It cannot be, my child. Go now with Cristine. I will come for thee very early tomorrow, I promise it."

Thanks to the strong habit of obedience, Arlette almost instinctively and without a perceptible effort put her hand within Cristine's, and quietly left the room. Had she guessed why they wished her to go, not so calmly would she have turned away without even one last look at the face of the dead.

Yet it was better that she should be spared the agonizing farewell, the bitter parting with the precious dust, even though the empty room looked so strangely cold and desolate next morning, and the sad surprise cost her more tears than she had ever wept before.

III

THE END

ALL THROUGH THE LONG SUMMER DAY the rain poured heavily and without intermission. Not far from what was even then the flourishing city of Cologne, in a very lonely spot, which could be reached only by intricate by-paths, stood a deserted and partly ruined barn. Its desolate appearance, and the silence that reigned undisturbed during the day-time, together with the unfrequency of light streaming through its windows in hours of darkness, would have given rise to no suspicions that it was used as a dwelling-place. Such was the case, although its only occupant was Arlette. She was one year older than when she watched beside her dying mother. She has mourned her mother, not alone as some children mourn, with sudden sharp gushes of sorrow, but also with quiet inner thoughts and silent tears, an utter lone-

liness stealing over her sometimes amidst her
play, or when she looked at beautiful scenes
or places, or even when she felt very happy.
For she was still a child, and not seldom a
happy and playful child.

Her father's watchful love had shielded
her as much as possible from the dangers and
hardships of their wandering life, and for a
thoughtful and imaginative nature like hers,
that life had its own peculiar and exquisite
enjoyments.

Even the necessity of passing whole days
in solitude did not press very heavily upon
her. There were weary and sorrowful hours,
but there were many bright ones too, for she
belonged to that class of children who can
surround themselves at pleasure with a fairy
world of their own creation.

As she sat on a bench in a corner of that
strange and crude dwelling, she busied herself with a goodly heap of field flowers, gathered on the previous day before the rain had
begun to fall. She did not merely arrange
them, nor did she throw them aimlessly
about as children so often do. They were
rather her playfellows than her playthings.
She talked to them, with them, for them, in-
vested them with ideal characters, made
them the heroes and heroines of a little
drama, which, to judge by her earnest face

and kindling eyes, she acted out with intense interest.

Suddenly recalled from her imaginary world to that of reality (though the one was to her nearly as unreal as the other), Arlette threw the flowers from her lap and rushed to the door. Two men, in dark serge robes and sandals, stood outside in the drenching rain.

She admitted them at once, though with a look of disappointment soon followed by an eager question, "Where is my father?"

"He comes soon, my little one," answered the elder, kindly. "Stand aside, child, lest we make thee as wet as ourselves."

"Ah, Father Heinz," replied the little girl, "I would I might have kindled a fire ere your return, but I durst not."

"Right, my child; it is not for such as thou to meddle with flint and fire."

"Not so," returned Arlette with a look of intelligence. "Oft have I kindled a fire; but my father said he feared the light might betray us."

"True, Brother Robert is always prudent. He would not have us venture the fire."

"Except in cases of necessity," said his companion, who stood yet upon the threshold wringing out his drenched garments.

"Cold winter nights were worse than this. What we bore then we can bear now," returned Heinz, betaking himself to the same employment, while Arlette hurried within to make what little preparations she could for their comfort.

"On such a night as this the flame could scarce be seen," rejoined Wilhelm, the younger of the two; "and we know not of any special cause for alarm."

Heinz shook his head. "Better to suffer wet and cold for a few hours, than to fall into the cruel hands of the townsfolk of Cologne."

"Better neither," said Wilhelm, who was still a young man, light-hearted and sometimes rather imprudent.

"Wait at least for Robert and for Father Johan, and let us hear their minds," said Heinz.

"Nay," returned his companion, "let us do it at once if it is to be done at all."

Heinz was accustomed to permit Wilhelm to take the lead in trifling matters, so after one more doubtful remonstrance, he allowed him to follow his own course, and the fire was soon blazing cheerily. If indeed there was danger, it seemed but slight and distant, while the comfort was present and very real. Wilhelm did not like discomfort. He would have borne torture and death without a murmur, rather than sacrifice one iota of what he believed to be the truth. But he felt keenly, and did not always so unmurmuringly en-

THE END

dure, the lesser trials of his wandering life, the daily privations that had nothing in them sublime or heroic, and which he sometimes forgot were just as much ingredients in the cup appointed for him as the dungeon or the stake.

They had not stood long drying their garments at the fire, and talking over their missionary work in the streets and alleys of the great town and the more secluded hamlets around, when the watchful Arlette sprang once more to the door, and joyfully admitted her father with the aged Johan, the missionary who had been the means of his conversion at Ghent, and who was, in fact, the patriarch of the little band.

Quick to observe the changes of the face she so loved, the little girl thought her father looked unusually grave and sad. He kissed her affectionately, but was very silent, scarcely speaking until their frugal supper was over, and they were all seated beside the fire.

Arlette was on his knee, Heinz sat nearest to him, and they soon began to converse in a low voice.

"Hast thou heard aught new today, brother?"

"No," returned Robert, "save that the townsfolk say —" It was not intended that Arlette should hear what the townsfolk said, for her father leaned over towards his companion and spoke in a whisper.

"Thinkest thou they have discovered our retreat?" A shade of alarm was visible in the speaker's face.

"I do not," said Robert quietly. "Yet it is possible."

"We ought then to abandon it without delay, and to seek another place of refuge."

"Such also is in my mind; for should they continue their search as they appear to have begun it, I have little hope they can fail in tracking us hither. At least, we are not safe."

"We are safe nowhere until the grave receives us," replied Robert sadly. But his countenance brightened as he added, "Rather should I say that nowhere are we aught but safe, since our Father reigns in Heaven, and the whole earth is His."

"True, but amidst our life of constant peril does thy heart never fail thee, Robert?"

"Cast down I have been sometimes, forsaken, never yet. And consider, friend, what comforts are given us, even in the midst of sorrow and disquietude. Consider the joy of bearing glad tidings to those who are pining in darkness and the shadow of death.

"Brother, today my footsteps trod for the first time the threshold of a lowly dwelling, one of the meanest in yonder great city. I found there alone, lying on a couch of straw,

The End

in a room more bare of comforts than even *this*, a poor girl, on whom death seemed to have already laid his hand. I spoke to her with sympathy and compassion, pitied her loneliness, and asked if she had no friend to watch by her side.

She said her sister tended her, but was obliged to spend the day in earning daily bread for both. So I knew there was time for me to speak and for her to listen, and I sat down beside her. I talked first of her bodily disease, of her symptoms and her sufferings, that I might unlock her lips and win her confidence.

Then we spoke of that other malady — the fatal sickness of the soul — and to my surprise and pleasure she understood me at once. God had shown her the great reality of *sin*, already. He had taken her by the hand and led her into the darkness after which the light cometh.

But she was seeking rest in prayers, in penances, and in all the mummeries of Rome and, of course, seeking it in vain. Thou knowest too, that men are not invited to buy the good things of the Church's providing 'without money and without price,' and with the awful fears of a soul conscious of unpardoned sin, and soon to stand in the presence of God, there mingled sordid calculations, mournful to hear, of how many nails could be wrung from their deep poverty to secure the good offices of the mass-priest.

Silver and gold, in truth, I had not; but what I had I gave her. Yet not I — what was I but the cup, the 'earthen vessel,' in which God was pleased to convey the living water to her parched lips? I told her the Saviour pardoned freely, that the redemption of her soul indeed was precious, but that He had paid its price, even to the last mite; and that, therefore, He could *give* remission of sins to those that came to Him. Hope and joy lighted up her wasted features as she seemed to grasp the great truth, that all was done for her. God willing, I shall see her again to-morrow; for, if I guess right, she has not many days to live."

He stopped rather abruptly, for the eager Wilhelm was detailing an interesting discussion he had held that day with an intelligent tradesman in the city, upon the virtue of relics and the use of pilgrimages. Whilst her father spoke, little Arlette drank in every word, and gave childhood's quick sympathy to the poor dying girl in Cologne. But she had not the same interest in Wilhelm's controversies, and soon her head pressed Robert's shoulder more heavily, and she sank into a sound and dreamless sleep.

Unwilling to be disturbed, she heard through her slumber confused noises around,

The End

and more than one low whisper close to her ear. But she soon started into full and terrified consciousness. Strange men, with scowling faces and drawn swords, seemed to fill the room, and with a cry of terror she clung to her father for protection. The look with which he met her frightened gaze awed and silenced her. It brought her back in thought to the room where her dead mother had lain and to her father's face as she had seen it then, full of an anguish unutterable, and to her incomprehensible. As in a dream she heard the rude voices of the soldiers, who poured in rapidly, and surrounded the little band of confessors.

"So we have stolen a march on ye at last, heretics," said one of the foremost among them. "Ye did not expect a visit tonight, I imagine, or ye would scarce have kindled yon fire to guide us."

She saw the unresisting Father Johan, his mild countenance calm as ever, seized and bound. She saw the impetuous Wilhelm almost throw himself among his captors, while with eager words he protested his readiness not to be bound only, but also to die for the Word of God and the truth of the gospel. She saw Heinz and her father standing side by side, with clasped hands, quietly awaiting the result, and as she looked once more on her father's face she saw that he saw only hers.

Could they touch him?

Then in a moment the thought flashed across her mind that this was martyrdom. Many times had she listened to stirring tales of those who for the Saviour's sake had borne and had patience even to the suffering of death. Many times did her young heart beat quick and fast, not with fear but with kindling enthusiasm, as the thought arose, "and I, too, may be a martyr."

And now the hour was come. Jesus would be with her, she knew. He had promised it, and she believed His word. Her father, too, would be there; she would hold his hand to the last. She had no terror therefore, save that these cruel men would let her live, would tear her away from him and leave her alone in that desolate place. One of them spoke in a low voice, "And this babe, what can she know of heresy? We care not to slay children."

"Oh, sir, take me with my father!" cried Arlette.

Robert's steadfast heart was wrung with anguish for her. He knew not what fate to dread most. It may have been he thought it best for her to accompany them to the city, and was not without a hope that her innocence might touch the hearts of their judges.

The End

So, held fast by him, she passed out into the darkness with the rest, after looking for one moment at the heap of withering flowers, for which an hour before she had cared so much. An hour was it? or a year, or many years? Or was it quite a different child, some little girl she had once known, but scarcely remembered now, who sat there in the barn playing with wild flowers. "I shall never play again," she thought, "for I am going to Jesus."

Then she was treading the long wet grass, the rain almost over, only now and then pleasantly touching her brow as if with a light cool finger. The way was dark as midnight could make it; but she felt quite safe, for she was holding her father's hand. It was all so strange, a wondrous dream, but on the whole a happy one.

"I am going to Jesus," still she thought; and although she felt vaguely that something very dreadful lay between — pain, death to be passed through, the river of death she had heard it called — she knew Jesus would bear her safely across, for was it not written, "He will gather the lambs in his arms"? Her ideas of suffering and death were indistinct and unreal, and her mind soon turned from them to the happiness and the glory beyond.

And now they were treading narrow miry lanes. Arlette grew weary, but cared little for that. Now they saw lights gleaming through the darkness before them. They were drawing near the city. Robert stooped down and spoke a few words of soothing and comfort to his little girl. She liked to hear his voice, but was too tired to answer.

In a little while the lights were all around them, shining from many a casement in the high houses, and reflected back from the wet, uneven street. At last they passed beneath a broad dark archway. They climbed a flight of steps. A door opened to receive them; then another door, which was closed and bolted as soon as they were admitted. They could rest, and not too soon for one of the party, who was scarcely conscious of anything save sleep. She was in her father's arms. She did not know he laid her gently down, and in hardly more than a minute, hope and fear, joy and sorrow, were all alike forgotten by her. No other closed in slumber in that prison room.

Two or three days afterwards, a plot of waste ground just outside the gates of Cologne was the scene of an impressive ceremonial. Thither the eager citizens crowded from every quarter of the town, some among them fierce and cruel, bigoted in their attachment to the Church, and rejoicing that the crime of heresy was that day to be purged with fire from their Catholic city; many without a distinct idea, simply wondering at all

THE END

they saw, and many more — yes, they were many, though they were scattered here and there in obscure places, and not for the most part known even to each other — sympathized with the innocent sufferers; some, indeed, would have given their own lives to rescue them. In vain, the priests were then all-powerful in Cologne, and they had their will.

Whatever the various sentiments of the dense crowd might be, there was a great silence as every eye turned to gaze on the victims, who were led bound towards the pile which had been erected in the midst of the place. Their demeanor, fearless but perfectly quiet and gentle, prepossessed the spectators in their favor.

"God help them," "God have mercy on their souls," was uttered aloud or breathed low by many voices.

"Waste not thy breath in prayers for yon heretic dogs," said a black monk to a woman near whom he stood, for there were many women in that crowd.

"Heretics or no," she answered stoutly, "they were good men and kind to the poor. My dying sister" —

"I would pity them as thou dost, good wife," interrupted a man, "had they been condemned by the council and the clergy for rash words uttered unawares, and without a chance for their lives. But the priests say they have each and all been offered a free pardon if they would but forsake their heresy. Yet are they obstinate enough to prefer death of the body and the soul together to leading Christian lives as good Catholics."

"Thou sayest truly, friend," rejoined the monk, "but what of thy sister, woman?"

"One of those clerks hath visited her, and spoken such good words of God and our Saviour that her heart was comforted within her. I think it was yonder tall, dark man with — blessed saints! what have they the poor child among them for? They cannot — no, they surely cannot intend that she should die!"

For little fair-haired Arlette stood among those doomed men, pale and calm, in her place beside her father, her hand clasped in his. After all it might be said that he endured the martyrdom for both. How could she comprehend or imagine its bitterness? At most it would be but a brief hour of anguish for her, perhaps not even that, for the good Shepherd indeed sometimes carries the lambs in His arms, so that their feet do not touch the waters of the dark river.

And now the hour had come, the pile was lit, and not one heart in the steadfast group gave way. In that crowd there were fathers and mothers too, in whose homes were loved and tender little ones like the martyr's child.

The End

They could not — they would not — see her perish.

An indignant murmur rose, nearer and nearer pressed the people, and at last strong arms seized the child, just in time, and dragged her from her place as the flames began to spread among the fagots.

"She is safe — thank God, she is safe!"

"Make the sign of the cross, poor child, and thank the saints for thy life."

"I cannot, I cannot! Let me go to my father!" wailed Arlette, while with all her little strength she struggled, struggled for death as others might have done for life.

"Where he dies, I must also die. Let me go, I cannot give up the Faith!" and an exceeding bitter cry accompanied the words.

"Back, back, good people! ye come too near the pile," shouted two or three of the officials, who were probably not unwilling to connive at the child's escape. But in the recoil that followed this order some confusion naturally occurred. The man who held Arlette, being rudely pushed by a neighbor, raised his hand to strike him. One moment's freedom for the child, and it was enough. With marvelous quickness she seized it. She reached the burning pile. She clasped her father's hand once more — yet once more — and now like a shroud the flames wrapped them around. A few minutes and all was over.

So Arlette won the victory, and so those five faithful martyrs of Jesus Christ passed that day to the crown prepared for them in Heaven.